PAPER-BAG COOKERY

LECTOR HOUSE PUBLIC DOMAIN WORKS

PAPER-BAG COOKERY

VERA COUNTESS SERKOFF

ISBN: 978-93-89679-38-0

Published: 1911

LECTOR HOUSE LLP
E-MAIL: lectorpublishing@gmail.com

PAPER-BAG COOKERY

BY

VERA COUNTESS SERKOFF

WITH NEARLY TWO HUNDRED RECIPES

1911

CONTENTS

INTRODUCTION.

"Paper-Bag Cookery" is the method of cooking food in a hot oven, having previously enveloped each article in paper, and thus cooking them in hot air and in the steam generated by their own juices. The method is fully explained and its advantages are clearly and incontestably set out in the following pages, but it may be well to sum up the latter succinctly in their order here that they may be taken in at a glance.

The greatest advantage of all is, of course, the great improvement in flavour and the retention in the food of its highest nutritive properties.

(1) **Food cooked in a paper bag is superior in flavour and of higher nutritive value than that cooked in any other way.**

The next advantage is its economy in time, in money, and in labour.

(2) **Food cooked in a paper bag loses practically nothing in weight.**

(3) **By cooking the entire dinner in paper bags in the oven an immense saving in fuel is effected.**

(4) **Food cooked in a paper bag takes, as a rule, a much shorter time to cook than when cooked by any other method.**

(5) **The entire meal may be prepared and placed in the bags overnight, thus saving considerable time during the busy morning hours.**

(6) **Joints require no basting, and provided care is taken to lower the gas sufficiently to prevent scorching the bags, the food can be left to look after itself until the proper time for dishing up arrives.**

A very great advantage both to mistress and maid is the cleanliness of the process. It is undoubtedly an advantage when doing without a servant to have no pots and pans to soil one's fingers, or to roughen one's hands with the necessary strong soda water for cleansing kitchen utensils.

(7) **No pots and pans to clean. No blackened saucepans to scour; no dishcloths to wash out, after washing the pots, thus saving soap and soda. The bags used in cooking are merely burned up.**

(8) **No constant and expensive renewal of pots, baking dishes, fireproof ware—frequently far from fireproof—tin saucepans burned through in no time—enamelled dishes from which the**

enamel so soon wears off. An ample supply of paper bags for an average family will cost at the utmost no more than sixpence per week.

(9) Comfort in kitchen and sitting-room. There is absolutely no smell of cooking during the preparation of meals, a very great advantage in houses where the kitchen is not completely shut off from the rest of the house.

(10) It is possible to cook all sorts of viands at the same time in paper bags. Even such articles as fish, onions, etc., can be cooked at the same time as the most delicate foods without impairing their flavour or imparting their own.

(11) Freedom from grease. Many dishes which are too rich for the digestion when cooked in the usual way may be put into a paper bag with no more butter than is necessary to grease the bag, and will be found to have gained in savour and delicacy of taste, while so completely free from grease that they will not disagree with the most delicate digestion.

(12) Meat is made tender by being cooked in a paper bag. Even if inclined to be tough, the same joint that, put into an oven and cooked in the usual way, would be almost uneatable, will, cooked in a paper bag, turn out surprisingly tender and palatable. The envelope keeps all the juices in, and thus enables the meat to be cooked to perfection.

(13) The juices which must in some degree run from meat, the syrup which may boil out from the fruit dumpling, the gravy which may exude from the meat pudding, are all preserved in the bag, instead of being lost in the baking dish or the boiling water, as would be the case if the bag were dispensed with.

(14) No scrubbing out of a greasy oven with dripping clinging to the sides; no washing out of the dripping pan or baking dish. A spotlessly clean oven is left, and when the bags have been burned up and the dishes washed, the cook's labours in connection with the finished meal are over.

(15) Even such articles which for some reason or other must necessarily be put into dishes, are immensely improved in flavour by being afterwards placed in a paper bag, and are also more equally cooked well as saved from all risk of burning.

PAPER-BAG COOKERY

CHAPTER I.

SHOWING THE ENORMOUS ADVANTAGES OF COOKING IN PAPER-BAGS OVER THE PRESENT METHOD.

WHEN Primitive Man first ventured on the daring experiment of applying heat to his newly-slain prey, he would most naturally adopt the obvious plan of suspending it on three sticks over a fire. The result, though no doubt to a certain extent tasty, would be smoked, charred on one side, raw on the other, and this, coupled with the frequency of burned fingers gained while rescuing the meat from the fire into which it fell when the sticks burned through, caused Primitive Man—or, more probably, Primitive Woman—to evolve the method of cooking known to us to-day as Paper-bag Cookery.

Paper not having been discovered, the prehistoric cook could not use the bags now placed at our disposal, but a very fair substitute was always ready to hand in the shape of green leaves, in which the meat was carefully wrapped. A hole was dug in the ground, and partly filled with large stones, on the top of which a fire was kindled. When it had burned out, the stones would be almost red-hot, and the meat, wrapped in the green leaves, was laid in, some of the hot stones being raked over the parcel, and then the hole was filled in with earth, so that neither smoke nor steam could escape. In fifteen minutes or so, or as near that time as Primitive Man could restrain his hunger, the meat would be done to a turn, and the hungry family would break open their primitive cooking oven, and devour the delicious morsels.

From Darwin's *Voyage of the Beagle* we learn that the Tahitians cooked their food at that date (1835) in precisely the same way, and those of us who have revelled in childhood in *Bill Biddon, The Trapper*, and other Indian stories, must remember the delightful feasts described in those books, where the hunters and their friends gathered round the camp fire at night, and ate buffalo meat and wild prairie birds in the same fashion. How much more delicious to the childish mind than the commonplace roast mutton of nursery dinners. In spite of the condescending explanations given by our elders that it was only the hunger of the hunters that made such cookery palatable, the child still believes in the delights of such a meal—and the child is right!

There is no method of cooking by which the flavour is so well brought out, and the juices so well preserved, as by cooking in this way; that is, by hot air surrounding the food, which is thus cooked in its own juices, and by the steam so generated.

Paper-Bag Cookery is not a mere craze of the moment; for once its advantages have been discovered, it will become firmly rooted as one of the best and most economical means of preparing food ever invented. Why it should have fallen into abeyance among civilised nations (except in the cooking of one or two special dishes) for so many centuries is impossible to surmise.

NO LOSS OF WEIGHT OR FLAVOUR.

One very great advantage of paper-bag cookery which will appeal strongly to the economist is the fact that meat thus treated loses little or nothing of its weight. To the great grief of the thrifty housewife, there is no way of preventing the lordly and expensive sirloin of beef or the dainty leg of lamb losing very considerably in its passage through the cooking process, and when one has paid a good price per pound for the meat, one certainly grudges losing even a few ounces of it.

In boiling meat less is lost, but even that little is mourned by the thrifty soul, and stews are recommended, because what is lost in the cooking goes to enrich the gravy and vegetables in the stewpan.

But stews, though nourishing and economical, are not savoury, and the thrifty housewife will rejoice to know that by placing her joint in a paper bag, her family may enjoy the savour and tastiness of roast meat, without the waste in the cooking. As the joint goes into the oven, so it comes out, the same weight, or, if in some instances there be some difference, it is so slight as to be infinitesimal.

Economy, however, is not everything, and paper-bag cookery appeals also to the epicure, who does not consider cost in ordering a meal to his taste.

Food cooked in a paper bag acquires a richness and a delicacy of flavour imparted by no other means of cooking. All the juices of the meat are preserved; there is no greasiness, no dryness, no risk of burning; even tough meat is made tender. Until a joint cooked by this method has been tasted, the epicure has no idea of the exquisite flavour and delicacy which await him.

HOW IT HELPS THE HOUSEKEEPER ON SMALL MEANS.

Quails, puff pastry, turbot, and salmon are all very well in their way, and it is gratifying to the wealthy epicure to know that to cook them in paper bags is to attain perfection; but there are many of us to whose limited incomes these dishes are quite unattainable luxuries, and who are more interested in knowing how to cook simple and cheap articles of food to advantage.

It is to these anxious housewives with limited purses that paper-bag cookery specially appeals; kippers, bloaters, and smoked haddocks are simple and cheap food, used every day as breakfast and supper dishes by those whose incomes oblige them to be careful in their expenditure. Excellent as these articles are, there are few more easily spoiled. They burn easily, and dry up very much in frying. A moment's neglect, and a burned, unpalatable, tasteless object is all that emerges from the frying-pan.

Cooked in a paper bag, however, there is no such danger and no one need fear to lose the savoury relish that a well cooked kipper or bloater possesses. They are just as tasty, but have acquired a flavour unsurpassed by any other method of cooking. The juices are preserved, and there is no fear of dryness. Place a kipper, bloater, or smoked haddock cooked in a paper bag before a lover of these fish, and he will discover new charms in his favourite dish.

No one can deny, however, that appetising as these homely fish are, the smell of frying kippers or bloaters is most aggressive. Not content with filling the house, it forces its way into the street, and triumphantly proclaims to our neighbours upon what humble fare we are feasting. But cooked in a "Papakuk Bag," there is absolutely no smell to reveal the nature of the coming repast, and as many people dislike very much the smell of the food they are about to eat, and, indeed, complain that the smell takes away their appetite completely, this in itself is a great gain.

THE PROPER BAGS TO USE.

Red mullet, cutlets, and one or two other dainties have always been cooked in paper (ordinary kitchen paper, thoroughly oiled), and it seems strange that the delicious flavour thus obtained did not earlier stimulate some observant and enterprising chef to apply the principle to other foods. But now that attention has been drawn to the matter, many of our best known chefs are strongly urging the use of paper bags. Joints of meat can be cooked by wrapping in sheets of kitchen paper, carefully secured to envelope the meat entirely, and exclude the air, but for other food bags are essential.

Let no thrifty soul think to economise by saving for this use the bags in which articles have been sent home from grocers, greengrocers, or other tradesmen. This plan would be an excellent illustration of the proverb, "Penny wise and pound foolish," for though a few pence might be saved, the spoiling of the food would be a much more serious expense. Cooked in these bags, everything would taste unpleasantly of paper, even if the cooking were otherwise successfully carried out.

A much graver matter would be the danger to health. The paper, not manufactured for cooking purposes, might have something injurious in its composition, or the paste used in joining the bags might contain some harmful substance, so that a doctor's bill would make the cost of the bags got without payment far in excess of those manufactured for the purpose, and sold for a very small sum.

HOW THE BAGS SHOULD BE FASTENED.

When the food has been placed in the bags, the openings must, of course, be secured, for the whole essence of this method lies in the complete exclusion of the air, and the sealing up of the juices and flavour of the food that it may cook in its own steam.

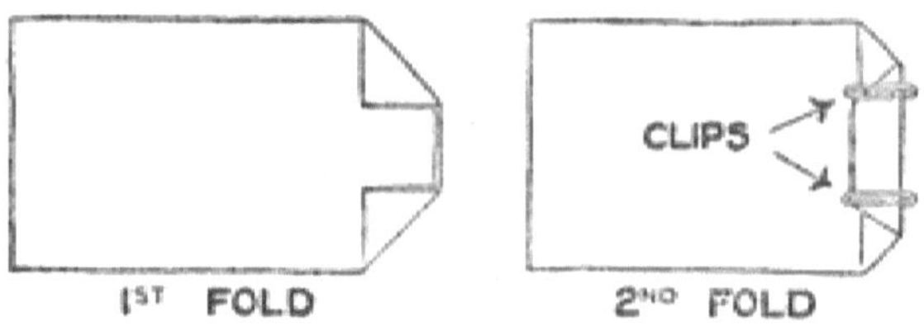

How to fix the clips.

Once the joint is in the paper-bag, the opening to the bag must be clipped down. First turn the corners down, as in the first fold, then bring the top of the bag over, leaving sloping corners. The clips can then be inserted.

Now, the question is, how to fasten the food in the bag in the most secure manner. Clips can be obtained with the bags, and these are excellent. Safety-pins are not advisable, as they are apt to tear the paper when being adjusted. On no account must ordinary pins be used, for they are easily overlooked when removing the paper, and lying unnoticed on the meat dish, might be conveyed to a plate and be inadvertently swallowed.

GREASING THE BAGS.

There is a great difference of opinion about this, some cooks greasing each bag inside and outside without any regard to what is being cooked; some grease only in special cases, and others do not use grease at all. It is, however, quite necessary to freely grease the inside of the bags containing fish or pudding, otherwise the food will stick to the bag, and although it is not wise to thickly grease one containing a joint, especially a fat joint, yet the meat itself should be lightly rubbed over with a morsel of dripping or vegetable lard to prevent the paper sticking to it. Butter should not be used, as it gives meat a bad colour.

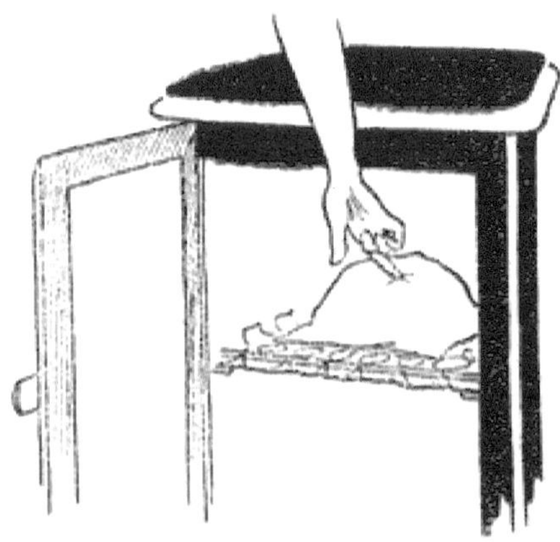

To find out whether the food is cooked, just press the bag with one finger. If it feels tender, it is quite all right.

If the bag containing a joint be thickly greased inside and out, the interior of the oven will be greasy and will smell, thus doing away with two of the benefits of paper-bag cookery—cleanliness and freedom from smell.

THE COOKING OF DIFFERENT DISHES TOGETHER.

If a joint of meat is being roasted in an oven in the ordinary way, nothing else may be cooked at the same time, unless it be a Yorkshire pudding or baked potatoes, which are placed below the meat expressly to catch the dripping and the gravy.

If the rash cook ventured to put in several articles of food at once, disaster would be the result. The tart would savour of roast pork, the meat taste of onions, or the baked fish would give its own special flavour to everything else in the oven. Apart from this, the heat required to cook the joint would curdle the milk pudding, and the gentle warmth required for the custard would leave the steak in an almost raw condition. Then, too, the necessity of hanging the joint from the bar at the top of the gas-cooker leaves very little room for anything else.

In paper-bag cookery, the most varied assortment of dishes will lie amicably side by side on the grid supplied with the gas-cookers, and no mingling of flavours or spoiling of one or the other will result. Cooking them thus altogether, an immense saving in time and in expense for heating is effected. Even the savoury onion will cook placidly by the side of a bag of gooseberries, without imparting its flavour to the fruit.

While cooking is going on, the oven door can be freely opened without risk of spoiling anything by the admission of cold air, which, of course, would be fatal to the contents of the oven in ordinary cooking.

THE CLEANLINESS OF PAPER-BAG COOKERY.

When dinner has been successfully cooked, dished up, and eaten, the labours of the cook are by no means ended, for then comes the distasteful business of clearing up. The oven must be cleaned while it is still hot, the interior well scrubbed out with hot water and soda to free it from the grease which will cause such an unpleasant smell next time the oven is used. The baking tin must next be attended to, and then comes the array of saucepans, stewpans, and frying-pans which have been used, and which are often so difficult to scour that one can understand and almost forgive the hard-driven "general" who puts them away in a dirty condition, trusting to be able to clean them some time before they are again required. In this particular, the contrast between paper-bag and ordinary cooking is most striking.

The meat having been cooked in a bag, there is no grease to be scrubbed from the oven, and none on the bars of the grid where it has lain; the interior of the cooker is perfectly clean; there is no baking or dripping-pan to be cleansed with hot water and plenty of soda; there are no saucepans to scour.

When the paper bags have been disposed of, there remain only the plates, knives, forks, and spoons to wash up, and that over, cook may sit down to rest.

This, in itself, is such an immense saving of labour and time, that the mistress who adopts "Papakukery" may be said to have gone far towards solving the servant problem.

THE BEST OVEN TO USE.

A gas-cooker is undoubtedly the best for paper-bag cookery, as the ease with which the heat is regulated, and a steady even degree maintained, the little attention it requires while the food is cooking, make it ideal for all ways of preparing food, but especially for the method now under consideration. Gas is absolutely perfection for paper-bag cookery. But all houses are not supplied with gas, and even if they are, the economical housewife may prefer to cook by coal fires, at all events in winter, when the kitchen-range is alight all day long, or when it is going for the purpose of getting hot water for baths.

An ordinary coal heated kitchen-range will answer very well for paper-bag cookery, if a little care and attention be given to the matter. The cook must firmly impress on her mind that the bags must *not* be laid on a solid baking sheet, but on a wire grid, which may be cheaply acquired at an ironmonger's; that the oven must be heated to 220° Fahr. before the food is put into it—a cooking thermometer is not an expensive item; and that, though the heat may be lessened after some twenty minutes, the fire must not be allowed to go down and then be built up again to complete the cookery.

If the bags are put on a hot baking sheet, the cooking will be a failure, because it is necessary for the hot air to circulate round the food and completely surround it; besides, the bags will burst as soon as they are laid on a hot solid surface.

When cooking in a gas oven, it must be remembered that the gas must be lighted and left full on for ten minutes before the food is put in, and also that the lower grid must not be put in the lowest groove, or the bags will catch fire from being too near the flame. The top grid should be put in the groove nearest the top of the oven, if that will allow the bags to lie conveniently on it, and the second grid as near the first as may be convenient.

A wire grid from the ironmonger's may be added to the two usually supplied with the gas-cooker; in some ovens there is room for two additional ones. After about ten to fifteen minutes, the gas may be turned half-way down, and this degree of heat steadily maintained till the cooking is completed.

Sometimes, when people are living in apartments, there is a supply of gas, but no cooker. In such a case, it would be easy to buy a gas ring and tubing to attach it to a gas jet. Over the ring a tin oven, such as can be had cheaply from most ironmongers, should be placed, and it will be found that a paper-bag dinner will emerge most successfully from it.

Even if nothing more than a paraffin stove is to be had, still the paper-bag cook need not despair. Longer time will be needed to get the oven placed on top of a paraffin stove to the necessary degree of heat, but by remembering this, and maintaining the same steady heat, paper-bag cookery may be managed much more satisfactorily in such an oven than ordinary cooking could possibly be.

A HOME-MADE GRID.

As a wire grid in the oven is necessary, and many housewives may not be able to try the new cooking because their ovens are not fitted with a grid, here is a very cheap and simple way of making a grid that will answer perfectly.

Get a piece of ordinary wire netting, cut it to the width of the oven, then thread through the natural edge on both sides an iron or brass rod—a curtain or stair rod will do—then place in the oven as shown in the sketch. The ends of the rods must rest on the little ledge in the oven which usually supports the iron shelf, and that will give the necessary strength and support to the grid. The total cost should not be more than twopence or threepence.

DISHING-UP.

At the end of the specified time, a peep into the oven will reveal the array of paper bags, probably well browned but not burned. If there has been the slightest smell of burning paper, it should at once be looked to and the gas reduced.

To remove the food from the bag.

Let the bag lie on a dish, take a pair of scissors and rip up one side
of the bag and also one end as shown by the dotted lines. Then
pull the bag away and the food will remain on the dish.

A large fish-slice should be employed to remove the bag containing the meat from the oven and place it on the hot dish ready for it. A pair of scissors should be at hand to slit open the bag, which must then be dexterously removed, leaving the nicely browned, perfectly cooked joint on the dish. There will be very little gravy, as that, of course, is the juice of the meat, and the claim of the paper-bag cookery is that it seals up the juices *within* the meat. On no account add water to the few spoonfuls of rich, strong gravy in the dish, for that would completely spoil the delicious flavour.

In families where much gravy is desired, it must be made separately with a little stock, browned and thickened.

The potatoes can now be turned out of their paper bag into a hot dish, and the same process can be followed with peas or sprouts. Cauliflower requires gentler handling. Its bag should be slit, and the nicely cooked flower—almost all green must be cut away—suffered to glide gently into a dish filled with hot white sauce ready prepared. The pudding may continue in the oven, the gas turned very low so that it may keep hot, but not cook any longer, till it is required.

CHAPTER II.

HOW TO COOK FISH.

THERE is nothing which is so delicious when cooked in paper bags as fish. Boiled fish is light and digestible, but most of the nutriment and flavour are lost in the water; and although less goes to waste when the fish is steamed or cooked in a conservative cooker, there is no comparison between these methods and paper-bag cookery. The flavour is unsurpassed; there is no smell of frying or boiling fat; no risk of burning; no spoiling by overcooking; no trouble or fuss looking out the right saucepan and bringing the fat to just the right degree of heat; in short, it is the perfection of fish cookery. It is an ideal way of cooking small fish or portions of fish. A salmon steak, cooked in a paper bag, is an epicure's dream, and no one who has not eaten one cooked in this way can form any idea of its exquisite flavour. Cod cutlet is a revelation, for it acquires a new and delightful flavour, while the cheaper and coarser fish, such as hake, rock salmon, monk-fish, etc., when treated in this way, gain so much in taste as to become real delicacies.

Skate is particularly nice cooked in a paper bag. This fish, though exceedingly wholesome and easily digested, has a rather strong flavour, which is objected to by many people. Oddly enough, this strong flavour entirely disappears when the fish is cooked in a paper bag.

SKATE.

A piece weighing about a pound should be soaked for about an hour in strong salt and water, then shaken free from moisture and rubbed over with butter. Season with salt and pepper and put into a well greased bag, with one tablespoonful of water and half as much vinegar. Cook for about eighteen minutes, and serve on a very hot dish, on which a slice of butter has been melted. This is a capital supper dish.

SALMON CUTLETS.

Take a slice of salmon weighing half a pound. Rub it over with butter which has been seasoned with pepper, salt, and a few drops of lemon juice, and put it into a very well greased bag. Have the oven very hot, and cook the salmon for fifteen minutes. Slit the bag with scissors, and slip the fish on to a very hot dish. This will have all the savour of fried salmon, but with a delicious flavour and aroma peculiarly its own. If the effect of boiled salmon be desired, put a scant half-teacupful of water into the bag with the fish.

FRESH HADDOCK.

Fresh Haddock is particularly dainty when cooked in this fashion. Have the fish cleaned and the head taken off. Rub both inside and out with butter, put it into a well greased bag with a tablespoonful of water, and cook for fifteen minutes. It will have the appearance of a boiled fish, and the curd-like whiteness and delicacy of its flesh will be extremely tempting, while the flavour will be far superior to that of a boiled haddock. Or, if a more savoury dish be preferred, the fish must be well dredged with flour, which has been highly seasoned with salt and pepper, then covered with bits of butter, put without water into a greased paper-bag and placed in a hot oven, the heat being maintained at the same degree for twenty minutes. The paper will become very brown, but must not be allowed to blacken or singe. The fish will then be a rich golden brown, closely resembling fried fish, but much more wholesome and digestible.

WHITING.

Whiting is very delicate cooked in a paper bag, and can be eaten by the youngest child or most delicate invalid without risk to the digestion. It is skinned, the tail fastened in the mouth, then placed in the greased bag with a tablespoonful of water, and cooked for about ten minutes. It is not so insipid as boiled whiting and is more nutritious.

KIPPERS.

Kippers are placed in a well greased bag, and cooked in a hot oven for about ten minutes. They should be very savoury, yet by no means dried up by this means of cooking, and are also not so rich as when fried.

BLOATERS.

Bloaters cooked the same way are quite as tasty as when fried, but lighter and more digestible.

SMOKED HADDOCKS.

Smoked Haddocks acquire a new and delicious flavour when cooked in a paper bag. They should be carefully wiped clean, well buttered, peppered, and put into a greased bag for ten minutes. A very nice variety is obtained by cutting a neat hole in the bag with scissors at the end of this time, carefully dropping in a couple of eggs, and returning to the oven till the eggs are cooked. Serve on a very hot dish upon which a good slice of butter has been melted. Or, put two or three eggs in a separate bag with a cup of water, and let them cook for six or eight minutes; serve in slices on top of the haddock.

FISH PUDDING.

Take equal quantities of cold mashed potatoes and cold cooked fish. Mix very thoroughly with two ounces of butter melted in two tablespoonfuls of milk to each pound of fish and potato, a saltspoonful of salt, half as much pepper, a pinch of dry mustard, and two hard-boiled eggs cut very small. Thoroughly grease a paper bag, put in the mixture, place in a hot oven, and cook for ten minutes.

RUSSIAN FISH PIE.

Roll out a short crust paste, made by rubbing three ounces of vegetable lard into ½ lb. of self-raising flour, and adding a well-beaten egg. Lay on this paste a thick layer of cooked rice; upon that put a layer of cooked fish, freed from skin and bone and pulled into flakes; upon that lay slices of hard-boiled egg, and another layer of rice. Season highly with cayenne pepper, salt, and a little grated nutmeg or ground mace. Just moisten with thick white sauce, nicely flavoured with a few drops of lemon juice, and cover with pastry, pinching the edges well together. Slip carefully into a thoroughly greased bag, and bake in a hot oven for fifteen minutes. This is extremely delicious.

FISH SAVOURY.

This is an original recipe, and is a very great favourite with most people. It requires special care and attention in making, but well repays the cook for any slight trouble it may cause her. It is also a capital way of using up cold fish and stale bread. Soak in cold water a little stale bread for an hour or two. Then drain and press very dry, beat up very thoroughly with a fork; season nicely with pepper, paprika if possible, salt, a very little ground mace or the zest of a lemon. Add cold fish, freed from skin and bone, and a well beaten egg. Mix all very thoroughly; have ready some ripe but firm tomatoes, cut off the tops, and scoop out the seeds and pulp. Fill the tomatoes with the fish mixture. Beat up some cooked rice with the pulp taken from the tomatoes, till it is a pretty red colour. Spread this coloured rice thickly on a very well greased paper bag, keeping the opening as wide as possible to admit the stuffed tomatoes, which must be embedded in the rice at equal distances. Bits of butter are put on the tops of each, the opening of the bag closed, and the bag very carefully slid into the oven and cooked for twenty minutes. Great care must be exercised in dishing up to preserve the appearance and shape of the dish. It is slid cautiously on to a hot dish, the bag slit and removed as dexterously as possible without disturbing the rice. If this is carefully done, the result will be a pretty as well as a remarkably savoury and appetising dish.

TINNED FISH.

The usual method of serving tinned salmon or lobster is to put it on a dish just as it is, though perhaps some more ambitious housewife may go the length of surrounding it with parsley, or even handing some salad with it. This is not very appetising; but as the fish is already cooked, it is difficult to warm it up without extracting all the flavour and nourishment left in it. Also, whether fried or baked or warmed up in the tin, it falls to pieces and presents a forlorn and unsightly appearance most untempting.

Now here is the chance of paper-bag cookery.

TO WARM UP TINNED SALMON.

Open the tin carefully, and drain off all the liquor. If it is in one firm solid piece, it will be best treated as salmon cutlet. Dust it lightly with pepper and salt, squeeze a little lemon juice over it, put it into a well buttered bag, fasten up very securely, and cook for six minutes in a very hot oven. Slide on to a very hot dish, dexterously remove the paper, and serve with white sauce. In appearance and flavour, it will be equal to fresh salmon. If the contents of the tin are in several pieces, however, it will be best to turn them into:—

SALMON CROQUETTES.

Open a tin of salmon, drain the liquor off, and turn the fish into a basin. Add an equal quantity of fine bread-crumbs, a little pepper and salt, a few drops of lemon juice, a tablespoonful of chopped cucumber, if at hand, and a well beaten egg, and mix thoroughly. Form into small flat rounds, and lay in rows on the well buttered bag, taking great care not to break them, and to keep them apart, otherwise they may run together in cooking. Secure the opening, and keep the bag perfectly flat as it is cautiously slid into the oven.

In such dishes, a large fish-slice is of great assistance in putting in and taking out of the bags the cooked food.

CURRIED LOBSTER.

Remove the lobster from the tin and cut it into nice pieces; add an ounce of butter, a finely chopped onion, a dessertspoonful of curry powder, and a small tea-cupful of stock already browned and thickened. Mix all well together, but avoid breaking up the pieces of lobster. Put into a thoroughly greased bag, and cook in a hot oven for twenty minutes. Turn into a very hot dish and add a squeeze of lemon before sending it to table. Serve with boiled rice and chillies.

LOBSTER CUTLETS.

Lobster Cutlets made from tinned lobster are very nice. Take the lobster from the tin, and pound it with an ounce of butter. Add half a saltspoonful of salt, the same of white pepper, and of ground mace. Beat all into a smooth paste, shape into neat cutlets, and cook in a well greased bag from six to eight minutes.

HOT LOBSTER.

Hot Lobster can be made from tinned lobster quite as well as from fresh. The lobster must be pounded exactly as in the previous recipe, salt, pepper, and mace being added in the same proportions; mix in about half as much fine bread-crumbs as there is lobster, or rather less, and moisten with two well beaten eggs. Beat the mixture thoroughly, make into a shape as nearly resembling a lobster as may be, or into a plain roll if artistic talent is wanting, cover with tiny bits of butter, put into a well greased bag with great care, and cook from eight to ten minutes. In dishing up, be very careful not to let the lobster crumble or break.

LOBSTER PATTIES.

Make some good paste with ½ lb. of flour, ¼ lb. of butter, and an egg. Roll out to medium thickness, and with a pastry cutter cut into small rounds. Mix in a basin a tinned lobster cut into pieces, four tablespoonfuls of thick white sauce, a teaspoonful of finely mixed parsley, a few drops of anchovy sauce, two or three of lemon juice, and a little cayenne pepper. Put small heaps of this mixture on half of the rounds, leaving the other halves to serve as lids to the patties, cover each with a lid, pinching the edges well together, and making them into scallops. Place in a buttered bag, prick the top of the bag with a skewer, slide into a hot oven, and bake from fifteen to twenty minutes. The rich golden brown of the pastry will contrast prettily with the lobster mixture, and this dainty dish will be as tempting in appearance as it is appetising in flavour.

MACKEREL.

Mackerel has the reputation of being a tasty but very indigestible fish. Paper-bagged, however, it retains its savoury nature, but loses its undue richness. It should not be washed, but wiped with a damp cloth, split open, seasoned with a little salt, pepper, and fine oatmeal, sprinkled with a few tiny bits of butter on the inner side, slipped into a greased bag, and cooked from ten to fifteen minutes according to size.

SARDINES.

Sardines are very appetising when cooked in a paper bag. Open the tin, and empty it, oil as well, into a bag. Do not grease the bag. While the sardines are in the oven, make buttered toast, which, it is perhaps needless to say, is one of the things which cannot be prepared in a paper bag. Cut the toast into strips and serve one sardine on each strip. They will take about five minutes in the oven.

KEDGEREE.

Kedgeree is a splendid breakfast dish on a cold winter's morning, and as it can be entirely prepared over night, saves much time and trouble in preparing breakfast. Grease a bag very thoroughly and abundantly; place in it equal quantities of cold cooked fish freed from bone and skin, and cooked rice, pepper and salt to taste, one ounce of butter, one teaspoonful of made mustard, and two chopped hard-boiled eggs. Mix very thoroughly. Next morning all that remains to be done is to get the oven hot, put in the bag and let it remain for ten minutes, when it will be ready to serve.

BRILL AND TURBOT.

Brill and Turbot are both extremely delicate cooked in paper bags. Clean the brill, cut off the fins, and rub it over with lemon juice. Put it in a well greased bag with half a teacupful of water, and cook it from fifteen to twenty minutes according to size.

Turbot, of course, must not have the fins cut off, these being a great delicacy, but otherwise it is cooked exactly like brill.

COD SOUNDS.

These must be soaked for an hour or two in strong salt and water, then very thoroughly washed and dried. They are then put in a paper bag with two table-spoonfuls of milk, and will take forty-five minutes to cook to perfection.

SALT FISH.

Salt Fish should be soaked for a few hours in water and a little milk, then wiped dry and put into fresh water with a quarter of a pint of vinegar in it, in which it must remain overnight. Next day, take it out, wipe it dry, rub it over with butter, and put it into a well greased bag. It will take an hour to cook.

EELS.

Small eels, such as are usually boiled, are most suitable for paper-bag cookery. Take four small eels, put them into a very well greased bag with one tablespoonful of water and a piece of butter the size of a walnut. Put into a hot oven for ten minutes, then turn the gas half-way down, and leave the bag for another twenty minutes. The eels will then be cooked to perfection, and of rich and delicate flavour. They should be served in a small tureen, and covered with parsley sauce.

EEL PASTY.

Eel Pasty is very delicious. A good crust is made from self-raising flour, butter, and an egg. Cut the pastry in two, and roll each piece into a pretty oval or round shape. Put the eels, cut into inch-long pieces, on the one half of the pastry; sprinkle them with minced parsley, a finely chopped onion, a little grated nutmeg, pepper, salt, and the juice of half a lemon. Cover over with the other piece of pastry, pinching the edges well together, and ornamenting them with a fork. Put into a very well buttered paper bag, and cook for an hour in a moderate oven. Have ready a very nicely flavoured thick white sauce, and when the pie has been removed from the bag and is on a hot dish, cut a hole in the upper crust and pour in the sauce.

FISH CAKE.

Fish Cake can be made from the remains of any cold fish. Pick the fish free from skin and bone, chop it finely, mix it well with equal quantities of bread-crumbs and cold potatoes, finely minced parsley, salt, and pepper. Make it into a cake with a well beaten egg, put it into a well greased bag, and cook for about half an hour in a well heated oven.

A COD'S HEAD AND SHOULDERS.

A Cod's Head and Shoulders cannot be better cooked than in a paper bag. Cleanse the fish thoroughly, and rub it well over with salt, which improves the flavour very much. Then wipe it dry and fill with a stuffing of bread-crumbs, chopped parsley, a small chopped onion, some grated suet, and a beaten egg. Rub the fish lightly over with butter, put into a greased bag, and cook forty minutes. The natural juices of the fish will form a sauce impossible to improve upon. A fresh haddock may be stuffed and cooked in the same manner, and is extremely savoury.

FRESH HERRINGS.

Fresh Herrings gain very much in flavour when cooked in a paper bag, and lose their oiliness. They are cleaned, wiped dry, split open, seasoned with salt, pepper, and flour. The bag is lightly greased to prevent the fish from sticking, but no butter or dripping must be put on the herring. Fifteen minutes will cook them to a turn.

PLAICE, SOLES, AND FLOUNDERS.

Plaice, Soles, and Flounders are simply brushed over with oiled butter, put into a well greased bag, and cooked for ten to twenty minutes according to size.

SEA BREAM.

Paper-bag cookery is ideal for bream. Well wash the fish, but do not have it scaled. Open it and fill with the stuffing recommended for cod's head and shoulders. Fasten it together again, wipe dry, and put into a greased bag. Cook for thirty minutes—longer if very large. Turn out on a hot dish, remove paper, scales, and skin; then place the bream on another hot dish on which a large piece of butter has been melted. Serve at once.

FISH STEW.

Fish Stew is an uncommon but very excellent dish. Small soles, flounders, dabs, and eels are capital cooked thus. Sometimes very small fish of this sort can be bought cheaply, but seem hardly worth cooking, and would be certainly cooked into mere dry scraps in ordinary cookery. Prepared in a paper bag, however, a very dainty meal may be made from them. Cleanse the fish and wipe them dry. Have ready a large bag, which has been sharply inspected and pronounced intact; well grease it both inside and out, put in the fish, cut in halves, or if very tiny, whole, if eels, cut into inch-long pieces. A mixture of the above-mentioned fish is better than if the stew consist of one kind only. Add half an onion cut into very thin slices, some finely chopped parsley, two cloves, one blade of mace, two bay leaves, a sprig of thyme, salt and pepper to taste. When this is all safely in the bag, pour in a cupful of stock, fish or meat stock, or if none is at hand, water will do, but whatever it is it must be slightly thickened. A small glass of port wine or claret is a great improvement. Close the bag very securely, and put into the oven for thirty-five minutes.

CHAPTER III.

HOW TO COOK MEAT.

Putting the joint into the bag.

This sketch shows how joints must be placed in the paper bag.
The bag should rest on the table; lift the uppermost edge, and
your food or joint can be slipped in.

PAPER-BAG cookery should appeal especially to the caterer for a small family. The difficulty of providing suitable joints for households of three or four persons is very great. A small piece of sirloin or half leg of mutton dries up to nothing when cooked in the ordinary way, and loud are the complaints that the flavour and juiciness of a large joint is not to be had under ten to twelve pounds of meat. Yet, if the housewife invests in the large, juicy joint desired, she finds it a very expensive business. One day's dinner hot and one cold is all that is really relished. Then follow the monotonous hash, the grill, the fried-up pieces, till everybody is tired of the eternal warmed-up dinners. If it is summer, probably a third of the expensive joint goes bad before it can be eaten up.

Cooked in a paper bag, however, the small joint is full as juicy and savoury as the eighteen-pound sirloin can be, while a dainty piece of loin of lamb is a delicacy which must be tasted to be realised.

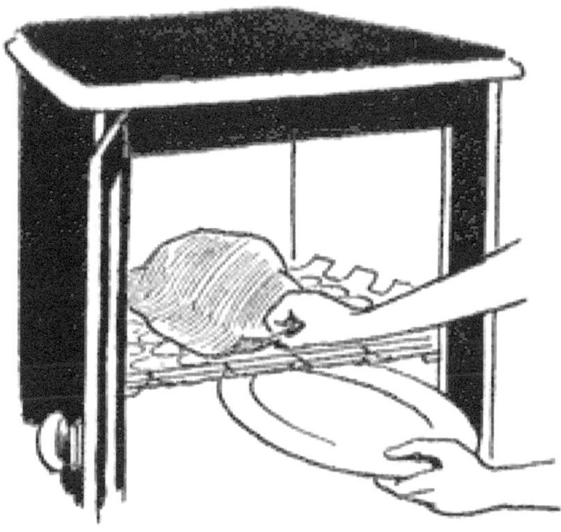

Taking the bag out of the oven.

The nose of the dish should be held about two inches under the grid. This allows the bag to be pulled out on to the dish.

LOIN OF LAMB.

Two pounds and a half or three pounds of loin of lamb will make a sufficient dinner for a small family of three or four persons, and leave enough cold to serve for supper. Wipe the meat over with a cloth dipped in hot water, and then with a clean dry cloth. Loin of lamb or mutton, being a fat joint, it is better not to grease the bag. Prepare a nice veal stuffing and lay it along the inside of the loin, drawing the flap over and skewering it to keep it in position. Put the meat in a good-sized bag; have the oven well heated; place the bag on the grid. Ten minutes later turn the gas about half-way down, and let it cook forty minutes longer, when it will be done to a turn, and be a rich golden brown.

SIRLOIN.

A piece of sirloin weighing between three and four pounds would not be worth eating if cooked in the ordinary way, but cooked in a paper bag it is a morsel for the gods. The bag must be greased and the joint lightly rubbed over with a little dripping. Forty-five minutes, ten with the gas fully turned on, should be sufficient for a joint weighing four pounds and under, unless liked very well done, when an extra ten minutes will not be found too much. If liked really underdone, it will be just right in forty minutes.

SHOULDER OF LAMB.

A small shoulder weighing three pounds or very little over is remarkably delicate, just the right size for a small household, and, cooked in a paper bag, is delicious. The butcher should be directed to bone it, and the cavity should be filled with a good forcemeat. Grease the joint over, but not the bag, and roast for fifty minutes, the gas being full on for the first fifteen.

ROAST VEAL.

Roast Veal is peculiarly adapted for paper-bag cooking, and a small fillet of veal makes a capital dish. The centre bone is taken out and the hole left slightly enlarged. The stuffing to fill this must be rather rich—a breakfastcupful of fine bread-crumbs, one ounce of grated suet, two rashers of fat, streaky bacon, finely minced, two or three oysters chopped coarsely, a tablespoonful of minced parsley, salt and pepper to taste, the zest of a lemon, and a well beaten egg. This must be firmly pushed into the cavity, and the joint then rubbed over with plenty of bacon dripping. Grease the bag thickly both inside and out. If the fillet weighs three pounds it will take an hour to cook, the gas fully on for ten minutes, then reduced one-half to finish.

ROAST PORK.

For a small family, a part of the loin should be purchased, a little stuffing of sage and finely minced onion introduced, and the joint cooked in a slightly greased bag, allowing twenty-five minutes to each pound. A roast leg of pork is also particularly well flavoured cooked in a paper bag. Stuffing may be introduced under the knuckle skin, or a savoury pudding (see chapter V.) may be cooked along with it. Both joints should be rubbed over with pure salad oil before being put into the bag.

ROAST CHICKEN.

Roast Chicken is a dainty morsel cooked in a paper bag. Nicely stuffed, it is rubbed over with butter and put into a well greased bag. Forty minutes is sufficient for a chicken. A large fowl will be tender and beautifully cooked in an hour.

GRAVY AND DRIPPING.

This is a very serious question. Many people are so devoted to gravy that, to quote Mrs. Todgers, in *Martin Chuzzlewit*, "a whole animal wouldn't supply them," and they will undoubtedly be disappointed in the amount of gravy got from a paper-bagged joint. In this method of cooking, the gravy stays in the meat, and that is what renders it so delicious, so juicy, so full of flavour. The meat which is dry and flavourless in proportion as its rich juices have been extracted, is the meat which yields most gravy. Therefore, paper-bagged joints yield very little gravy, and to add any water to the few spoonfuls of rich, strong gravy they do yield would be to spoil the flavour utterly. When the bag is opened, the small quantity of gravy and dripping within must be poured into a basin, the fat skimmed off, and the remaining gravy added to some gravy made from stock, and kept hot in readiness, poured into the gravy-boat and sent to table.

There will be very little dripping, for the same reason as there is very little gravy, but the mellowness of fat cooked in a paper bag is quite indescribable, therefore the scanty supply can be no very great drawback.

TINNED FOODS.

Tinned foods fill a very important part in housekeeping. It is a great convenience to have some tins of various preserved foods in the store-room for use in emergencies. The butcher may fail to call, a downpour of rain prevent a shopping expedition, or guests may unexpectedly arrive on a "finish-up" day, that institution so dear to the heart of the thrifty housewife, who so contrives the fragments of the larder that they form a sufficient meal for the household without leaving a crumb over. In all such emergencies it is very comforting to know that the larder is well furnished with tinned foods of reliable brands.

Then, again, tinned foods are the great stand-by of people living in apartments. There is little accommodation for storing food, and it is not pleasant to keep meat, even for a few hours only, in the room where one sits; in summer it becomes an impossibility. The landlady may be obliging enough to offer the use of her safe, but there are obvious drawbacks to this arrangement. Therefore, tinned foods are frequently brought into use, and prove very handy to the lonely woman in lodgings, or the small family living in apartments. Still tinned foods are not very appetising. Served cold, they neither look tempting nor taste savoury, especially on a winter's day; heated in the tin they acquire an unpleasant "tinny" flavour, recooked as stews, or put into a hot oven, they lose all flavour and nutritive value. So utterly do they lose their distinctive taste that it is impossible to tell beef from mutton, rabbit from chicken. It is in such cases that paper-bag cookery proves itself invaluable. A dish specially to be recommended is

MINCED STEAKS.

It is put up in tins costing elevenpence halfpenny each, and one tin will make an ample dinner for four or five persons, or provide several meals for one. The method of cooking is simplicity itself.

Well grease a good-sized bag, both inside and out, turn the mince out of the tin into the bag, with no additions of any kind. Put into a hot oven for fifteen minutes. Serve with a border of cooked rice (see chapter IV.), and any vegetable preferred. This is a delicious dish, the flavour and juice so well preserved by the method of cooking that it cannot be distinguished from mince made from rump steak.

ROAST BEEF.

Roast Beef is rather insipid served cold from the tin, and is flavourless recooked in the tin. Turned out, however, thickly spread with roast-beef dripping, put into a thoroughly greased bag, laid in a very hot oven for fifteen minutes, and served on a hot dish with small paper-bagged tomatoes (see chapter IV.), it is exceedingly nice.

ROAST MUTTON.

Roast Mutton is prepared in the same manner, but small onions cooked in paper bags may be substituted for the tomatoes.

TINNED RABBIT.

Tinned Rabbit is best served as curry. Well grease a paper bag. Turn the rabbit out of the tin (it will probably be rather broken and the flesh be separated from the bones), and put into the bag in neat pieces. Add two finely minced onions, a cooking apple cut in dice, the juice of half a lemon, and a teacupful of stock, browned and thickened and with a dessertspoonful of curry powder stirred smoothly into it. Fifteen minutes in a hot oven will be sufficient for this.

TINNED CHICKEN.

Tinned Chicken is very nice curried like the rabbit. Or it may be fricasseed. Turn it out of the tin, add a teacupful of white stock, thickened with arrowroot and seasoned with salt, pepper, and a little ground mace or nutmeg, a finely minced onion, a few young carrots, and turnips cut into dice, and a few green peas. Put into a well-greased bag and lay in a hot oven for fifteen minutes.

BAKED MUTTON IN CRUST.

This is a particularly delightful way of cooking mutton, for it retains all the juice and flavour of the meat, and is exceedingly light and digestible.

Choose a nice solid piece of mutton, the fillet end of the leg is the best. Make a good suet crust, using beef suet and water; roll it out to about a quarter of an inch in thickness; it must not be too thin. Keep it a square shape, and make it large enough to contain the meat and completely cover it. Place the meat in the centre of the crust, which neatly fold over it, pinching the opening well together after damping, and sprinkle flour over it. Then thickly grease a paper bag large enough to hold it easily, and gently slide it in. If the meat weighs about four pounds it will take about an hour and a half to cook, the oven being very hot at first, and the heat reduced by half after ten minutes. This dish is extremely nice, the meat particularly juicy and tender, and the crust superior in flavour to that cooked in any other way.

THE HOMELY IRISH STEW.

The Homely Irish Stew is admirable cooked in a paper bag. Buy two pounds of small neck of mutton chops, trim nicely and take away excess of bone and fat. Cut two or three small onions into rather thin slices, and two pounds of potatoes into thick slices, sprinkle meat, onions, and potatoes with herbs finely rubbed to powder, salt and pepper to taste, add a large breakfastcupful of water. Fasten the bag very securely, and cook in a hot oven for one hour. Turn into a very hot dish.

HARICOT STEAK.

Take a pound and a half of good steak, with no gristle or sinew in it. Cut into neat pieces about two inches square. Chop an onion finely, cut several tomatoes in slices and add these, also some green peas, and young carrots and turnips cut in dice. Rub a teaspoonful of "Bisto" smooth with a little water, and add it to a break-fastcupful of water. If any sour milk is at hand, a tablespoonful of this will be a great improvement. Tie together a bay leaf, a few sprigs of parsley and thyme, and put this in also. Put all the materials into a good-sized paper bag, which has been well greased, fasten very carefully, and cook in a hot oven for forty-five minutes.

STEAKS.

It has been said that a steak grilled over an open fire is the perfection of steak, but that is merely because steak cooked in a paper bag has not yet become known. Well grease a paper bag, put in a pound of rump steak cut in a thick slice, and put on the grid in a hot oven for about fifteen minutes.

CHOPS.

Chops are daintier and more savoury done in a paper bag than in any other way. Choose loin chops, trim them very nicely, and lay side by side in a well greased bag. Put in a hot oven and cook for about fifteen minutes.

BEEF OLIVES.

A pound of beefsteak cut into neat slices, longer than broad, makes a nice dish of beef olives. Mix a nice stuffing of two ounces of grated suet, two of bread-crumbs, a tablespoonful of minced parsley, a little ground mace, pepper and salt to taste, and a well beaten egg. Spread each olive with this, roll up, tie with string, lay tidily in a greased bag, put in a hot oven and cook for forty-five minutes. Serve on a very hot dish, with a pat of *Maître d'hôtel* butter placed on each olive.

BEEFSTEAK PUDDING.

Make a nice suet crust with finely chopped or shredded suet, self-raising flour, and water. Roll it out to a medium thickness, and cut it in two. Shape both pieces into a neat round. On the one round lay a pound of steak cut into small pieces rather larger than dice; add two sheep kidneys cut small, season with salt, pepper, a finely minced onion, a tablespoonful of flour; add a teaspoonful of vinegar or lemon juice, and a tablespoonful of water. Cover with the other piece of crust, pinching the edges well together. Put into a greased bag, and cook in a hot oven for about forty-five minutes.

IMITATION HARE.

Mince one pound of beefsteak with half a pound of raw fat bacon, add half the quantity of bread-crumbs, salt and pepper to taste, a teaspoonful of anchovy sauce and a well beaten egg. Form into a neat shape, slide into a greased bag, and cook forty minutes.

A CARPET BAG.

This is an uncommon and very delicious dish. Choose a large thick steak in one piece and of equal thickness all over. Cover it thickly with small plump oysters, roll it up, secure each end, put it into a greased bag, and cook it in a very hot oven for forty-five minutes.

INDIAN CURRY.

Cut the meat, mutton, steak, or poultry into small pieces; peel and chop an onion very finely, mix with the juice of half a lemon, pepper and salt to taste; add a cup of sour milk, in which a dessertspoonful of curry powder and one of flour have been mixed smooth; put it into a large bag, and cook for forty-five minutes.

PAPER-BAGGED RABBIT.

Cut the rabbit into neat joints, add a bunch of sweet herbs, two finely chopped onions, three cloves, three whole allspice, half a teaspoonful of black pepper, a thinly cut piece of lemon rind, two tablespoonfuls of mushroom ketchup, and two rashers of fat bacon cut in dice. Add a teacupful of stock, thickened and browned, and put into a well greased bag. Cook in a hot oven for forty minutes, if the rabbit is young and tender. If not, an hour will not be too much.

KIDNEYS.

Kidneys are delicious cooked in a paper bag. Take four sheep's kidneys, cut in two, take out the core. Wrap each kidney in a thin slice of fat bacon. Put into a well greased bag, and cook in a hot oven for twelve minutes.

KIDNEY STEW.

Skin and trim the kidneys, remove the core, cut into quarters. Roll each piece in flour, highly seasoned with salt, pepper, grated nutmeg, and a little dry mustard. Place in a greased bag with a tablespoonful of minced onion, half as much minced parsley, and a teacupful of stock, browned and thickened. Thirty minutes in a hot oven will cook this.

LIVER AND BACON.

Cut a pound of sheep's liver into small pieces, dip each in seasoned flour, wrap round with a very thin piece of fat bacon; put into a greased bag with two tablespoonfuls of water and a teaspoonful of lemon juice. Cook from fifteen to twenty minutes.

MINCE COLLOPS.

Mince one pound of beefsteak very finely, dust with a little flour and season with salt and pepper. If liked, a finely minced onion may be added. Put this in a greased paper bag with half a teacupful of water, and cook for twenty-five minutes.

SAUSAGES.

Put a pound of pork sausages into cold water for five minutes. Then take them out and strip off the skins. Put them in a lightly greased bag, and cook them for twelve minutes. As a pleasant variety, two or three tomatoes, skinned and cut in halves, may be cooked in the same bag, and are excellent. Other savoury breakfast dishes are: —

ANGELS ON HORSEBACK.

Take some very thin slices of bacon, lay an oyster on each, secure, and put in a well buttered bag. Six minutes will cook these nicely.

HAM AND EGGS.

The national breakfast dish is greatly improved by being cooked in a paper bag. The required number of rashers are put into a bag in a hot oven, and after six minutes a hole is cut in the paper and the eggs dropped carefully in. As soon as they are set, which will be in a few minutes, the dish is ready for serving.

EGGS.

Eggs put into a bag with a cup of water, and placed in a hot oven for four to five minutes, are superior to those cooked in a saucepan.

DRESDEN PATTIES.

Take some slices of stale bread and cut out rounds of about two inches in diameter. Scoop out the centre to form a deep cavity. Dip these in a thick batter. Have ready a mixture of minced cooked chicken and ham, stirred to a thick paste with white sauce. Fill the rounds with this, put into a buttered bag, and cook ten minutes.

SAVOURY EGGS.

Put into a paper bag as many eggs as may be required, add a cupful of water, and put into a hot oven for fifteen minutes. Take out and drop into cold water. When cold shell and cut them in halves lengthways; take out the yolks, and pound them with minced ham, minced parsley, salt, pepper, and butter. Return the mixture to the whites, press firmly together, brush over with oiled butter, put into a greased bag, and return to the oven for five minutes.

SCOTCH EGGS.

Proceed with the eggs as in the previous recipe, but cut the cooked eggs in halves across, not lengthways. Have ready sausage-meat mixed with a raw beaten egg. Lightly flour the halves of the eggs, and wrap each half in sausage-meat, rolling into the shape of a ball. Put into a buttered bag, and cook twelve minutes.

POTATO SURPRISE.

Take six raw potatoes, wash and peel them, and scoop out a good deal of the inside; fill with nicely minced meat (cooked or raw), chopped parsley, salt, pepper, a little butter, and a tablespoonful of tomato sauce. Put into a greased bag, and cook from thirty to forty-five minutes, according to size.

SCOTCH WOODCOCK.

Take a dessertspoonful of Yarmouth bloater-paste, a tablespoonful of cream, a piece of butter the size of an egg, the beaten yolks of two eggs, and a little cayenne pepper. Mix all very thoroughly, put into a buttered bag, and cook five minutes. Have ready hot buttered toast cut in strips. Spread each strip with the paste and serve very hot.

EPIGRAMS.

This is a very savoury breakfast dish and easily made. Cut neat slices from a cold leg of mutton. Spread them with Strasbourg meat or any nicely flavoured potted meat that may be at hand. Make a very thick batter with four ounces of flour, one tablespoonful of oil (or oiled butter), pepper, salt, a gill of milk, and an egg. Press two slices together, thus making a sandwich, dip into the batter, and place in a well buttered bag. Do this with all the pieces, arranging them side by side in the bag, but a little apart, that they may not run together in the cooking. Slide cautiously on to the hot grid, without disturbing them, and cook fifteen minutes. Serve on a very hot dish and immediately, for they lose their lightness very quickly.

CHAPTER IV.

HOW TO COOK VEGETABLES.

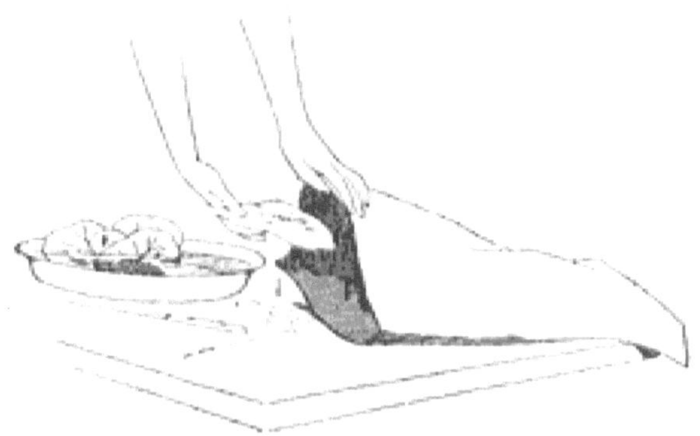

Preparing to cook cabbage.

THOSE who have tried the foregoing recipes are unanimous in their approval, but as regards the cooking of vegetables in paper bags, opinions are divided. Several noted vegetarians are enthusiastic on the subject, and declare that paper-cooking is the very best possible way of conserving the juices and flavour of all vegetables. Others, again, shake doubtful heads, though they admit that some vegetables are improved by this method of cooking, while others are quite decided against it, maintaining that a new and unpleasant flavour is imparted to vegetables so cooked. On investigation, however, it will be found that these last-mentioned critics have not given paper-bag cookery a fair trial. They have probably seized on the homely cabbage as an inexpensive subject on which to experiment, hastily washed it, thrust it into a paper bag, and placed it in the oven for an indefinite period. The result, naturally, is uneatable. Shredded very finely, and put into a well buttered bag with a cup of water, a piece of butter the size of a walnut, pepper, and salt, a palatable dish will emerge from the oven. At the same time, cabbage, plainly boiled or cooked in a conservative boilerette, is in many people's estimation a more superior dish. Potatoes, again, are a cause of division in the camp. They undoubtedly acquire a new flavour when cooked in a paper bag, and this flavour is not agreeable to every palate. Many people prefer new potatoes plainly boiled, for the young, immature vegetable is of so watery a nature that unless the moisture be dispersed by rapid boiling, the potato is too wet and waxy to be palatable. For this reason, new potatoes cooked by steam or in a conservative boilerette are seldom liked, and paper-bagged new potatoes are open to the same objection. It is a different matter, however, with old potatoes, which, when cooked in a paper bag, are very generally liked, and several excellent and proved recipes for cooking old potatoes in paper bags are given further on.

Asparagus is not always a success cooked in a paper bag. Some people complain that the flavour is by no means so delicate when so treated as when simply boiled or cooked by steam or in a conservative boilerette, therefore this vegetable is best put on the black list.

Other vegetables which have been tried and found wanting are celery, turnip-tops, and artichokes. These, however, when once boiled, can be utilised to make many delightful dishes in paper-bag cookery. It may, too, be worth the while of the ardent paper-bag cook to continue to experiment with them until success crowns her efforts. Speaking personally, these vegetables have not met with general approval when cooked in paper bags. But one cannot waste time in lamentations over the few vegetables which are failures cooked in this way, when one considers how many there are which gain so much in flavour as to be a revelation in delicacy and richness of taste to those who have only known them cooked in the ordinary way.

Green peas gain a perfectly exquisite flavour when cooked in a paper bag, but a certain amount of care is required. Too much water will ruin them, and if left too long in the oven they will be hard. One family declared with one voice against paper-bag cookery, because a dish of young, fresh peas emerged from the oven looking like tiny brown bullets, and crackling crisply between the teeth of those who tried to eat them. But this, of course, was the fault of a careless, incompetent cook, not of paper-bag cookery.

Broad beans are delicious cooked paper-bag fashion; but here, also, care and attention are required, as also with French beans and scarlet runners. Tomatoes cooked in this way are infinitely superior to those cooked in any other way, and there are a great variety of delicious tomato dishes to be cooked in paper bags. Young carrots and turnips gain in flavour so cooked, and cauliflower paper-bagged is unsurpassed. Brussels sprouts are not without merit, and mushrooms, onions, cucumber, and vegetable marrow gain so much in flavour as to almost fulfil the harassed housewife's aspiration for a new discovery in vegetables.

POTATOES.

Pare and wash the required number of potatoes and place in the greased bag wet from the washing. Put in a hot oven and cook for fifty minutes, reducing the heat after ten minutes.

STEWED POTATOES.

Stewed Potatoes are a very savoury dish. Wash and peel as many potatoes as are wanted, cut each into four thick slices, and put in a greased paper bag, with a finely chopped peeled onion, a tablespoonful of minced parsley, a good piece of roast-beef dripping, salt and pepper to taste, and half a cup of water. In forty minutes turn this savoury and delicious potato mixture into a very hot dish and serve at once.

DUCHESS POTATOES.

This is an excellent way of using up cold mashed potatoes. Melt a piece of butter or dripping in a little milk, the quantities being in proportion to the amount of potato; add pepper, salt, a pinch of dry mustard, and beat all very thoroughly up together. Butter a bag very thickly, put in the potato, and cook in a hot oven for ten minutes.

SLICED POTATOES.

Slice the potatoes thickly, wash well, and then dry in a cloth. Sprinkle with salt and a little flour. Butter a "Papakuk" bag very thickly, and cook for thirty minutes. The bag must be shaken now and then to make the potatoes crisp.

GREEN PEAS.

Shell the peas and to each half peck add a pinch of salt, one lump of sugar, and one leaf of mint; more than one leaf would give too strong a flavour to the peas. Add one glass of water, and cook for three-quarters of an hour. The gas should be reduced after five minutes. If the heat is too great, the peas will be hard.

BROAD BEANS.

Remove the pods and then shell the beans. This extra trouble is quite worth taking, for it makes all the difference in the delicacy of the flavour, and the skins are very easily removed. Put the beans when skinned into a thickly buttered bag, add a piece of butter the size of a walnut, into which has been worked a tablespoonful of flour, a little salt, and a teaspoonful of minced onion. Add also a cupful of water, and cook three-quarters of an hour, reducing the heat after the first five minutes.

DUCHESS GREEN PEAS.

Shell the peas and put into a thickly buttered bag with a lettuce cleaned and pulled into very small pieces, a few spring onions, a leaf of mint, a pinch of salt, a little castor sugar, a good slice of butter, and a cupful of water. Cook for about three-quarters of an hour, the gas turned down after the first five minutes.

FRENCH BEANS AND SCARLET RUNNERS.

These are excellent cooked in a paper bag. Contrary to the opinion of many cooks, the beans should never be sliced, but cooked whole. If the scarlet runners are very large and coarse, they may be cut into two or three pieces, but otherwise, they should merely have the tops and stringy parts removed and be cooked entire. Put them into a well buttered bag, with a slice of butter, a tablespoonful of minced parsley, the same of minced onion, if the flavour is liked, the juice of half a lemon and half a teacupful of water. Cook for about thirty minutes.

CARROTS.

Wash and scrape a bunch of young carrots, and put them into a buttered bag, with half a teacupful of milk and water. Cook for twenty minutes. If the carrots are large and no longer young, they should be cut into thick slices.

TURNIPS.

New turnips are delicious when cooked in a well buttered paper bag. Wash and peel them, cut into thick slices, put into a greased bag, with half a cupful of milk and water, a pinch of salt, a pinch of castor sugar, and half a teaspoonful of white pepper. Cook for about thirty minutes.

MUSHROOMS.

These are particularly good cooked in a paper bag. They must be freshly gathered, if they are to be really nice. Cut off a portion of the stalk, peel the top, and wipe the mushrooms carefully with a piece of flannel and a little salt. Put them into a buttered bag, with a piece of butter on each mushroom. Cook for twenty minutes. This method preserves all the aroma and flavour of the mushroom.

CAULIFLOWER.

There is no more delicious way of cooking a cauliflower than by cooking it in a paper bag. Cut away all the green, carefully cleanse the cauliflower, cutting the stalk crosswise to secure equal cooking. Lightly butter the cauliflower all over, put very carefully into a bag with half a tumbler of water, and cook thirty minutes.

PARSNIPS.

Wash, pare, and cut into slices as many parsnips as may be required, sprinkle with salt and pepper. Put them into a greased paper bag, with a cup of water and a little thickened milk. Cook for twenty minutes.

ONIONS.

The onion is rich in nitrogenous matter, induces sleep when taken at night, and is excellent as a remedy for colds. It has a soothing action on the nerves, and is beneficial to the kidneys. Take moderate-sized Spanish onions, remove the outer skin; cut off the tops to form lids, and hollow out a little of the onion. Fill this with sausage-meat, cored and skinned sheep's kidney, or a little minced and seasoned meat. Rub over with dripping, put into a well greased bag, and cook for an hour.

ONIONS AND TOMATOES.

These two vegetables go particularly well together. One excellent method of cooking them is to take as many tomatoes as there are onions, slice off the tops, scoop out some of the pulp, and carefully fix them in the hollow of onions, which have been steamed till tender and a hollow scooped in each. Put a piece of butter in the tomato centres, drop an egg into each, sprinkle with salt and pepper, add a tiny bit more butter, replace the top of the tomato, cover with the piece of onion previously cut off, put into a well greased bag, and cook for fifteen minutes.

TOMATO STEW.

Take nice ripe tomatoes. Plunge into boiling water for a few seconds, then put into cold water for the same length of time. Take them out and pull off the skins, which will now come away readily. Cut them up roughly in a basin; add salt and pepper, the grated rind of half a lemon, a bouquet of herbs, thyme, parsley, and bay leaf, and half a teacupful of water, and a piece of butter. Mix together, and turn into a well buttered bag. Cook for twenty minutes. Empty into a hot dish, pick out the bouquet of herbs, and serve immediately.

TOMATO PIE.

Prepare the tomatoes as in the foregoing recipe, and put into a basin roughly cut up. Mix in a tablespoonful of chopped onion, salt, and pepper, a teaspoonful of grated lemon rind, half a cupful of weak stock or water, a tablespoonful of fine bread-crumbs, a small piece of butter. Have ready macaroni boiled and cut in inch-long pieces. Mix with the tomato. Thickly butter a "Papakuk" bag, put in the pie, and cook for twenty minutes.

STUFFED TOMATOES.

This is a very nice supper or breakfast dish. Choose ripe but firm tomatoes. Cut off the tops, and put them aside. Scoop out the seeds from the tomatoes, and fill with a little minced cooked meat, nicely seasoned; or cut a sheep's kidney in four and use it as stuffing; or a pork sausage skinned and made to fit the hollow. Put a tiny piece of butter on each, sprinkle with salt, pepper, and a little minced parsley; fit on the lids, brush over with oiled butter, put into a greased "Papakuk" bag, and cook for twenty minutes.

VEGETABLE MARROWS.

These are particularly good cooked in "Papakuk" fashion. Plainly boiled and served with white sauce, it is an insipid vegetable, and even mashed with butter it is not very savoury. Prepared, however, in the following method, it is both tasty and satisfying. It is best pared before being cooked, although many vegetarians maintain that by doing so a great deal of the flavour and juice is lost, an assertion made also of the cucumber. This is very true when either vegetable is cooked in the ordinary way, but not so in paper-bag cookery. Having peeled the marrow, it must be cut in two, lengthways, and all the seeds and fibres removed. The cavity must be filled with a tasty stuffing of minced onion, cooked meat, finely minced, and half as much bread-crumbs seasoned with salt and pepper, and also some minced parsley, chopped beef suet, and a well-beaten egg. Tie the two halves together with thin string, brush over with oiled butter, put carefully into a thickly greased bag, and cook forty-five minutes.

SLICED VEGETABLE MARROW.

Peel a rather small marrow, and slice it into rings, cutting out all seeds and fibres. Sprinkle each ring with salt and pepper. Have ready a very thick batter, dip each ring in this, and put it, with as much batter as it will take up, into a very thickly buttered bag, and cook thirty minutes.

SAVOURY VEGETABLE MARROW.

This is a very tasty vegetable dish. Peel, cut open right through the middle, not lengthways; take four or five ripe tomatoes, plunge first into boiling, then into cold water, to remove the skins, then cut up roughly in a basin, add two onions, finely minced, a teaspoonful of lemon juice, salt and pepper to taste, a slice of butter or some grated suet, any remnants of cold ham or bacon there may be in the house, finely minced, a teaspoonful of minced parsley, half a cupful of fine bread-crumbs. Bind the mixture with the yolk of an egg, well beaten, and fill in the two halves of the marrow. Carefully put each half in a separate well buttered bag, the mixture side uppermost, and cook for forty-five minutes.

CUCUMBER.

Simply peel one or more cucumbers, brush over with oiled butter, season with salt, pepper, sprinkle over with a little flour, put into a well buttered "Papakuk" bag, and cook twenty minutes.

CUCUMBER FRITTERS.

Peel a young cucumber, cut in slices of a medium thickness, season with salt, pepper, the juice of a lemon, and leave them to soak for an hour. Have ready a thick batter, dip in the slices, sprinkle with minced parsley and a little minced onion, put into a thickly greased bag and cook fifteen minutes.

CUCUMBER STUFFED.

Peel a large thick cucumber, cut off the top, scoop out the seeds, fill with a mixture of minced cold meat, a few bread-crumbs, seasoning, and a little stock to moisten. A very nice stuffing is made with some sausage-meat or some kidneys cut small, flavoured with minced onion and parsley. Fix on the top with white of egg, brush over with oiled butter, sprinkle with bread-crumbs, and cook twenty minutes in a thickly greased bag.

Cereals do not seem very adaptable for paper-bag cookery, but with a little care and attention they lend themselves very fairly to this method of cooking, and gain considerably in flavour thereby.

BUTTER BEANS.

Butter Beans are extremely nice cooked in paper-bag fashion. They want a great deal of soaking to be really mellow. Wash the beans well, and put to soak early in the morning in abundance of water. Leave all day. By night the beans will have absorbed most of the water. Pour off any that may remain, leaving them quite dry. Cover the basin and leave till morning. This gives the beans a much nicer flavour than if they were cooked at once. Next day skin them. They are much superior when the outer skin is removed, and the trouble is really trifling. Put them into a buttered bag with a cupful of water, a sprinkle of minced parsley, a tablespoonful of minced onion, two rashers of fat bacon, cut into dice, but no salt, which would render them hard. They will be ready in an hour and a half. If the skins are left on, they will take another half-hour. Have ready a little butter, just melted over the fire, season with salt and pepper, and pour over the dish of beans before sending to table. If the bacon is omitted, substitute a good slice of butter in the bag.

LENTILS.

Either Egyptian or German lentils are excellent in a paper bag. Wash them well, soak all night in abundance of fresh, cold water. Next day put them in a well greased "Papakuk" bag, with the water in which they have been soaking, a carrot, a turnip, a parsnip, and an onion, chopped up roughly. Add neither salt nor pepper. Cook two hours, and they will then be tender enough to press through a colander. Season the resulting *purée* with salt and pepper, re-heat, and serve as a vegetable. Or add enough boiling stock to make a thick cream, stir in carefully a well beaten egg, and serve as soup.

LENTIL CUTLETS.

Cook the lentils as in the recipe already given. When they have been pressed through a colander, add enough bread-crumbs and mashed potato to make a stiff paste, season rather highly with salt, pepper, a little lemon juice, and a tablespoonful of onion juice. Mix thoroughly, form into neat cutlets, place in a thickly buttered bag, and cook fifteen minutes.

RICE.

Well wash a cup of rice, and put to soak overnight. Next day put it with the water in which it has soaked and at least another cupful into a very thoroughly greased bag. If it is not sufficiently greased, the rice will stick to it. Cook thirty-five minutes.

SAVOURY RICE.

Soak a cup of well washed rice overnight. Next day put it into a well greased bag with a sliced onion, two skinned and cut-up tomatoes, pepper, salt, a piece of thinly cut lemon rind, a couple of rashers of streaky bacon cut in dice. Add a cupful of stock or water and cook thirty-five minutes.

VEGETABLE ROLL.

Mash a quarter of a pound each of cooked carrot, turnip, vegetable marrow, haricot beans, and potatoes. Season with pepper, salt, grated nutmeg, mixed herbs; mix all well, bind with a beaten egg, form into a shapely roll, put into a greased bag, and cook fifteen minutes.

SAVOURY MACARONI.

Cut cold boiled macaroni into convenient lengths, and put into a basin. Skin and cut up roughly two or three ripe tomatoes; tinned may be used when fresh ones are expensive. Add these to the macaroni; add also a tablespoonful of strong gravy or some made from "Lemco" or any good meat extract; pepper, salt, a chopped onion, half a cup of fine bread-crumbs, and the zest of a lemon. Put all into a well buttered bag and cook fifteen minutes.

GROUND RICE FRITTERS.

Rub ground rice smooth in a little milk, and add enough to boiling milk to make a thick paste. Add to this a tablespoonful of onion juice, a piece of butter the size of a walnut, pepper and salt to taste, and a tablespoonful of grated cheese. Mix well and let it get cold. Form balls out of the paste, put into a well buttered bag, and cook fifteen minutes.

MUSHROOM PUDDING.

Roll out a nice short crust, cut it in two. On one half lay small button mushrooms, properly cleansed; sprinkle with a little salt and pepper; put bits of butter over them, cover with the other half of pastry; put into a buttered bag and cook fifteen minutes.

TURNIP CUPS.

Take nicely shaped round turnips, cut off the tops and scoop out some of the centres; fill with green peas, put little bits of butter on the tops; put the cups carefully into a well greased bag, so as not to upset them. Add cautiously about two tablespoonfuls of water and cook twenty minutes.

ONION DUMPLINGS.

Take as many onions as may be required, peel them, and make a deep incision across them; put into this cut a piece of butter or dripping, salt, and pepper. Make a good short crust, roll it out, and cut into as many pieces as there are onions. Put an onion on each, and work up the paste as if making an apple dumpling. Put into a well greased bag and cook about an hour.

CHAPTER V.
PUDDINGS AND CAKES.

With the exception of soup, an entire dinner can be cooked in "Papakukery" fashion, and, apart from other advantages, it will gain immensely in flavour and nutritive value from being thus cooked. Almost all puddings and sweet dishes can be cooked in paper bags, and are much improved in taste and goodness.

APPLE PUDDING.

Peel, core, and slice the apples. Make a good short paste crust, roll it out to a medium thickness; lay the apples neatly on one half, cover thickly with castor sugar, add the juice of half a lemon, squeezed over the apples; fold over the pastry, pinching the edges well together; put into a well greased bag and cook fifteen minutes.

APPLE PUFFS.

Make half a pound of the finest flour perfectly smooth by passing it through a sieve. Roll half a pound of fresh butter in a cloth to free from moisture; rub a piece into the flour with the finger-tips very thoroughly till it quite disappears; add a well beaten egg, and roll out the paste on a stone slab with a glass rolling-pin; a clean round bottle will answer if the only household roller is of wood. Put more butter in tiny bits over the paste; dredge lightly with flour; fold it up and roll it out; let it stand three or four minutes. Repeat this, leaving it a few minutes each time, for four or five times. Then roll it out and cut into square pieces. Lay a few slices of apple on each, cover with castor sugar and a little ground cinnamon, fold half the paste over, point to point, forming a triangular puff. Put the puffs into a buttered "Papakuk" bag and cook fifteen minutes.

APPLE DUMPLINGS.

A plain, not too rich, paste crust is best for these. With a corer extract the core from the whole, unpared apple, which is less likely to break than one which has been peeled. Fill the hollow with powdered sugar and a little ground cinnamon, if the flavour is liked; a little ground ginger makes a nice flavour, with the zest of a lemon or a pinch of mixed spice according to taste. Divide the paste into as many neat rounds as there are apples, put one apple on each round, work the paste smoothly over, wetting the edges to make them adhere. Place them in a well buttered "Papakuk" bag and cook in a moderate oven for forty minutes.

STEWED APPLES.

Stewed Apples are best cooked in a shallow tin or pie-dish, though they can be cooked placed simply in a well buttered bag. The apples are sliced, add a little lemon juice, sugar to taste, and a small quantity of water. Place in a well buttered bag, or put first into a pie dish which is slid into a bag—the last is really the best way. With or without the dish, cook for half an hour. The oven, after the first five minutes, must not be very hot.

ECONOMICAL BREAD PUDDING.

Put about a pound of stale bread into a basin and just cover with cold water. Leave it for an hour or two; or overnight, if more convenient. Drain off the liquid, pressing the bread in a colander or a vegetable presser; or press with the hand until free from moisture. Put into a basin, add two ounces of moist sugar, a quarter of a pound of cleaned sultanas or raisins, a teaspoonful of mixed spice, and one well beaten egg. Beat very thoroughly, put into a thickly greased bag, and cook forty minutes.

BREAD PUDDING.

This is a richer pudding than the foregoing, but is very light and digestible. Put stale bread to soak in just enough cold milk to cover. When quite soft, beat it well up, without pouring off any of the milk which may not have been absorbed by the bread. Add a quarter of a pound of sugar. Put into a well buttered bag and cook forty minutes.

GOOSEBERRY PUDDING.

Three breakfastcupfuls of bread-crumbs are mixed with half a pint of gooseberries and quarter of a pound of brown sugar. A little spice may be added, if liked. Mix in two ounces of butter or grated suet; beat in one or two eggs. Put into a well buttered bag and cook forty-five minutes. Reduce the gas by one-half after the first five minutes.

LEMON DUMPLINGS.

Lemon Dumplings are made exactly in the same way as the foregoing, substituting the juice and the grated rind of one large or two small lemons for the gooseberries, and mixing with one egg only. Form into balls, adding a little flour if the mixture is not sufficiently firm. Place into a buttered bag and cook for about fifteen minutes.

JAM ROLY-POLY.

This favourite nursery pudding is never so dainty as when cooked in a paper bag. In this way there is no risk of the jam "boiling out," to the disappointment of the little people to whom the jam is the chief part of the pudding. Make a nice, but not too rich, crust from vegetable lard and self-raising flour. Roll it out to an oblong shape, spread over with any kind of jam preferred, leaving a good two inches clear all round. Roll up the pudding very carefully, securing the edges by wetting and sifting flour over. Put in a thoroughly greased bag and cook thirty minutes. If any jam should chance to ooze out, it will be retained in the bag, and should be poured over the pudding when in the dish.

RAISIN BLANKET.

This is another nursery favourite. Roll out a light paste crust, as directed in the foregoing recipe. Sprinkle it over with large raisins, stoned and cut in halves; cover with a thick layer of brown sugar; squeeze the juice of a lemon over; roll up, secure the ends, put into a well buttered bag, and cook thirty minutes.

RICE PUDDING.

For this pudding use flaked rice. Bring a pint of milk to the boil, add an ounce of loaf sugar, stir in one and a half or two ounces of flaked rice and boil a few minutes whilst stirring; take from the fire and allow to cook. When nearly cold, add two well beaten eggs, put into a thickly buttered bag, and cook thirty minutes, the heat of the oven being reduced after five minutes to less than half. Have ready a dish in which a layer of stewed fruit or jam has been placed, and turn the pudding out on the top of this.

TAPIOCA PUDDING.

Flaked tapioca should be used for this, and it should be made in exactly the same manner as rice pudding. Both these puddings, and also semolina and ground rice, can be poured first into a buttered dish, and the dish put into a "Papakuk" bag. This secures a good appearance for the pudding, without losing the advantages of paper-bag cookery.

FRUIT TARTS.

Fruit Tarts can be made in the ordinary fashion, and the dish containing the tart can be put into a bag to get the full advantages of the method. Or they can be made without dishes. Either a short crust or puff paste may be used, as may be preferred. The paste is rolled out to a medium thickness and cut into two ovals or rounds. On one is laid the fruit—gooseberries, rhubarb, apples, black currants, red currants, and raspberries, or any suitable fruit in season—sweeten the layer of fruit with castor sugar. A little lemon juice, a pinch of ground ginger, or cinnamon, are considered by many people to improve the flavour of rhubarb and apples, and a very little sherry is thought to bring out the flavour of red currants and raspberries, but much less flavouring of any kind is required in paper-bag cookery, for the bag retains the flavour so perfectly that it is easy to overdo any strong flavour.

The fruit is then covered with the other piece of paste, pinch the edges of paste together, and ornament to taste; put into a well buttered bag, bake for about twenty to twenty-five minutes, and serve with castor sugar sifted over.

STRAWBERRY GÂTEAU.

A sixpenny sponge or Madeira cake is the foundation of this summer sweet. Cut the top neatly off, scoop out a deep hole, saving the cake to be used in making a Cabinet pudding. Fill the cavity with ripe strawberries, cover with sifted sugar put on the top; pour over the whole a glass of sherry, mixed with a tablespoonful of strawberry syrup, and one of lemon juice. Let it stand to soak for a few minutes, then put it into a well buttered "Papakuk" bag, and place in a hot oven for ten minutes. Take out and serve at once, handing custard or whipped cream with it.

CABINET PUDDING.

Bring one pint of milk to the boil, stir in a cupful of cake-crumbs. The pieces cut out of the cake used for the Strawberry Gâteau will be sufficient, finely crumbled. Stir for a few minutes, then lift off the fire, and when slightly cooled, add the well beaten yolks of three eggs, a quarter of a pound of raisins, cleaned and stoned, a quarter of a pound of candied peel, two ounces crystallised ginger, and two ounces of butter. Beat all together very thoroughly, put into a well buttered bag, and cook forty-five minutes, reducing the heat by half a few minutes after putting in the pudding. Beat up the whites of the eggs with a little sifted sugar and a few drops of essence of vanilla. When very stiff, pile it on the top of the pudding and serve at once.

PLAIN SUET PUDDING.

This pudding, whether intended to be eaten with meat or with jam or treacle, is infinitely superior cooked in a paper bag to the same pudding boiled or steamed. Mix one pound of self-raising flour with four ounces of chopped suet, preferably vegetable, and a pinch of salt. Mix to a stiff dough with water, put into a buttered bag and cook for forty-five minutes. This has quite a different flavour from a boiled suet pudding.

SIMPLE PLUM PUDDING.

Two heaped breakfastcupfuls of self-raising flour, one cupful of chopped suet, one cupful of raisins, stoned and cleaned, one of prunes, chopped and stoned, a little finely cut candied peel, one beaten egg, and enough milk to mix to a very stiff dough. Put into a well buttered bag and cook for about fifty minutes.

ROBIN TARTLETS.

Make a short crust paste, roll out, line some little patty pans, and fill with this mixture: one ounce of butter, melted, two ounces of ground rice, three ounces of castor sugar, one well beaten egg, a few drops of almond essence, or a spoonful of minced almonds. Put these into a "Papakuk" bag and cook fifteen minutes.

GERMAN GOOSEBERRY PUDDING.

Two cupfuls of flour, two of bread-crumbs, four ounces of chopped suet, one teaspoonful of ground ginger, one pint gooseberries, washed, topped, and tailed, and two tablespoonfuls of golden syrup; mix all well together, and make into a very stiff dough with a little milk; put into a thoroughly greased bag and cook for an hour.

PALESTINE PUDDING.

Mix six ounces of self-raising flour, four of sultanas, four of chopped suet, four of brown sugar, one dessertspoonful of ground cinnamon. Beat up one egg with two tablespoonfuls of milk, mix to a stiff dough. Put into a well buttered "Papakuk" bag and cook forty-five minutes.

DATE PUDDING.

Mix six ounces of bread-crumbs, four of self-raising flour, three of grated suet, half a pound of dates, stoned and chopped, but no sugar. Moisten with a beaten egg, and, if necessary, a little milk, but do not make the mixture liquid. Put into a greased bag and cook for an hour.

LANCASHIRE ROLY-POLY.

This is a nice variety of a favourite children's pudding. Make a good short crust and roll it out into an oblong shape. Cut two apples into small pieces, and mix thoroughly with two ounces of sultana raisins, two tablespoonfuls of golden syrup, a teaspoonful of mixed spice, a little grated lemon rind. Spread this mixture on the crust to within an inch of the edge; roll up, pinching the sides well together in the process. Put into a greased bag and cook for an hour.

PINEAPPLE PUDDING.

Bring one pint of milk to the boil, sprinkle in enough flaked sago to make a thick batter. Cook for a few seconds. When cool, add the beaten yolks of three eggs, an ounce of castor sugar, and a teaspoonful of vanilla essence. Butter a "Papakuk" bag very thickly, pour in the pudding, and cook gently for thirty minutes. Meanwhile, open a tin of pineapple rings and lay them in a dish. Empty the pudding on the top of this; have the whites of the eggs whisked very stiff with a little icing sugar and a drop or two of vanilla essence; pile this on the top of the pudding and serve at once.

SAGO PLUM PUDDING.

Soak four tablespoonfuls of fine sago all night in a breakfastcupful of milk. Next day add a teacupful of bread-crumbs, two of self-raising flour, one of best raisins, cleaned and stoned, the grated rind of quarter of a lemon, one ounce of butter (melted), and a well-beaten egg. Put into a thickly buttered bag and cook one hour.

RAISINS.

This simple dish is much liked by children, and is very wholesome and nutritious. Choose large, fine raisins, put them in a buttered "Papakuk" bag with a cupful of water, and let them cook for about forty minutes. They are excellent for children, eaten with bread and butter, and act as a gentle laxative.

PRUNES.

These are also excellent for children. Wash the prunes carefully, then let them soak all night in enough water to cover them and the juice of a lemon. Next day add two ounces of sugar to a pound of prunes, put them into a greased bag, with the water and lemon juice, and cook forty-five minutes. This is also a pleasant and gentle laxative, and is generally much liked by children.

LEMON PUFFS.

Grate the rind of two fresh lemons, mix with ten ounces of castor sugar. Beat the whites of two eggs to a stiff froth, and whisk all together to a very thick paste. Form into dainty balls, and place some distance apart in a thickly buttered "Papakuk" bag, and cook fifteen minutes.

CASTLE PUDDING.

Beat one ounce of butter and half a cupful of castor sugar to a cream; add three well beaten eggs, and beat all well together. Then sift in gradually one breakfastcupful of self-raising flour and mix thoroughly. Put into a thickly buttered bag and cook for about thirty minutes.

QUINCES.

Core and cut into slices six quinces, put them into a greased "Papakuk" bag with two teacupfuls of sugar and one of water. Cook for three hours in a slow oven. They will then be tender and of a beautiful rich colour. They are not often met with, but cooked thus are a delicious fruit.

CAKES.

Cakes are very dainty, and gain in flavour and richness when cooked in a paper bag. Many are cooked simply in the bag, but others must be put into a greased tin and then enclosed in the bag.

LADIES' FINGERS.

Ladies' Fingers are nice little cakes for afternoon tea. Beat two eggs very lightly, add one teacupful of sugar and a little essence of lemon. Add enough self-raising flour to make a firm dough. Roll out, cut into strips, put into a buttered bag, and cook fifteen minutes.

GOLDEN CAKES.

Beat half a pound of butter to a cream, add six ounces of sugar and the yolks of three eggs, and beat well; then put in three ounces of chopped orange peel and one pound of self-raising flour. Mix well, divide into buns, put into a well greased bag, and cook twenty minutes.

SHORTBREAD.

Shortbread is delicious cooked in a paper bag. The following is the recipe of an old Ayrshire cook whose shortbread is always considered unsurpassed. It is very rich, however, and the amount of butter may be reduced by one-half if considered extravagant or indigestible; but if the recipe be followed exactly, a very delicious cake will be the result.

Rub one pound of butter into one pound of flour. Rub it until it is like bread-crumbs. Then add a quarter of a pound of sugar and gradually work into a dough, which can be rolled out thickly, cut into fancy shapes, put into a buttered bag, and cook for twenty minutes. If half a pound of butter to one pound of flour be used, the dough must be moistened with one beaten egg and two tablespoonfuls of cream. The first recipe, however, is for genuine Scotch shortbread.

DOUGH CAKE.

Get the baker to bring half a quartern of bread dough. Beat into it quarter of a pound of butter, half a pound of sugar, a quarter of a pound of sultana raisins, two ounces candied peel. Let it stand for half an hour, put it into a buttered "Papakuk" bag, and cook one hour.

TEA-CAKE.

Mix three-quarters of a pound of self-raising flour, half an ounce of butter, and a cup of milk into a light dough; roll out, cut into round cakes, slip into buttered bags, and cook fifteen minutes.

YORKSHIRE TEA-CAKES.

Cream the white of one egg in as much butter and sugar together; beat into the white of the egg as much ground rice and self-raising flour; mix to a light dough with one tablespoonful of milk. Butter two plates, spread over the mixtures, put each plate into a "Papakuk" bag, cook fifteen minutes, spread one cake with warmed jam, put the other on the top, and serve hot.

COCOANUT BUNS.

Beat a quarter of a pound of butter and a quarter of a pound of sugar to a cream, then beat in two eggs, quarter of a pound of desiccated cocoanut, and one gill of milk; stir in a quarter of a teaspoonful of ground ginger and three-quarters of a pound of flour; butter some patty pans, half fill with the mixture, put into "Papakuk" bags, and cook twenty minutes.

SPONGE ROLL.

Beat four eggs and one cup of sugar together for five minutes, stir in one cup of self-raising flour, put into an oblong greased tin, enclose this in a "Papakuk" bag, and cook ten minutes. Turn out and spread with heated jam, and roll up at once.

AMERICAN COOKIES.

Put four tablespoonfuls of sugar into a basin, pour over it three tablespoonfuls of melted butter, mix well together; beat two eggs with two tablespoonfuls of milk and stir in; add as much self-raising flour as will make a very stiff dough. Roll out a quarter of an inch thick, cut with a pastry-cutter into nice rounds, brush each over with milk, sprinkle thickly with sugar, slip into well buttered bags, and cook twenty minutes.

LUNCH BUNS.

Beat well together one egg, half a cup of sugar, and one teaspoonful of butter, add one cup of self-raising flour, and mix very thoroughly. Form into buns, put into a well greased bag, and cook fifteen minutes.

CHERRY CAKES.

Beat a quarter of a pound of butter and two ounces of sugar together till very light, add one egg, very thoroughly beaten, stir in by degrees half a pound of self-raising flour. Turn the dough out on a board; chop two ounces of dried cherries finely, blanch and chop one ounce of sweet almonds. Roll out the dough, sprinkle over the cherries and almonds, and fold the dough together; roll it out again and fold it again; roll it out once more to half an inch in thickness; cut into rounds; put into a thickly buttered bag and cook ten minutes.

NURSERY TEA-CAKES.

Mix well together half a cup of butter, one of sugar, half a cup of milk, two of self-raising flour, two teaspoonfuls of vanilla essence, two well beaten eggs. Shape into buns, put into buttered bags, and cook twenty minutes.

CROPPER CAKES.

Beat three ounces of butter to a cream with three ounces of sugar; put half a pound of self-raising flour into a basin, and add it by slow degrees to the butter and sugar. Add a well beaten egg and a few drops of essence of vanilla. Make into a smooth dough, form into small cakes, place into a well buttered "Papakuk" bag, and cook fifteen minutes.

FEATHER CAKE.

Beat half a cup of butter to a cream, add two cups of sugar, and beat well; add one cup of milk with one tablespoonful of baking soda dissolved in it; three eggs, the yolks and whites beaten separately, one cup of flour with two teaspoonfuls of cream of tartar mixed in it; then add two more cups of flour without the cream of tartar. Beat very thoroughly. Put into a well buttered tin; enclose the tin in a "Papakuk" bag and cook forty-five minutes.

GINGER CAKE.

These are particularly wholesome for children, and are an agreeable laxative.

Take one pound of self-raising flour, and rub it well together with a quarter of a pound of sugar and half an ounce of ground ginger; then add half a pound of golden syrup and a tablespoonful of honey. Melt three ounces of butter in a quarter of a pint of hot milk; dissolve a teaspoonful of carbonate of soda in the milk and add it to the other ingredients. It must be a very stiff dough. Form into flat cakes, slide into very thickly buttered "Papakuk" bags, and cook forty-five minutes.

CHAPTER VI.
MISCELLANEOUS RECIPES.

FOR those who still hesitate whether to adopt paper-bag cookery or not, it may be as well to repeat the solid advantages of this method. For one thing, it minimises labour and saves time, thus going far to solve the servant problem. The cook who has not the never-ending labour of cleaning saucepans and baking-tins, who has leisure for reasonable rest and recreation, is a contented being, not likely to give notice at awkward moments. The expense of most labour-saving domestic utensils prevents their adoption in households where means are limited, but the bags necessary for paper-bag cooking cost the merest trifle.

Only those who live in small houses or flats know the misery of having each meal heralded by a violent smell of cooking, which invades every room, and robs the average person of all appetite; the tenant of those uncomfortable dwelling-places known as "Maisonettes" knows only too well what it is to inhale the fragrance of the downstairs burned onion or frying bloater; while the occupants of the lower maisonette suffer from audible and pungent remarks upon the odours from their kitchen, remarks which frequently lead to friction. Now, paper-bag cookery does not smell.

Paper bags are cheap. The young couple setting up modestly in life are spared the outlay of an expensive range of cooking utensils; the occupant of cramped apartments has not to endure the obtrusive little kitchen in bed-or sitting-room, and the thrifty housewife has not the continual necessity of replacing a worn-out saucepan or burnt-out frying-pan. And these things run into money. All that is necessary for the equipment of the up-to-date paper-bag cook is, of course, a kettle for boiling water, a conservative boilerette (Welbank) for the cooking of these few dishes not amenable to paper-bag treatment, and an egg saucepan. For though eggs are delicious cooked in a paper bag, it would be an extravagance to light the oven up for that purpose alone. Perhaps a frying-pan might also be included, but the rest of the kitchen outfit may consist entirely of "Papakuk" bags.

DOING WITHOUT A KITCHEN.

With the aid of paper-bag cookery, the up-to-date householder may eliminate the kitchen altogether, thus gaining another room. The small flat at a moderate rent usually consists of one sitting-room, two bedrooms, a kitchen, and a bath-room. It is equally unpleasant to sit in the room in which one has just dined, or to take meals in the room where they have just been cooked. With a little contrivance and ingenuity, the kitchen may be transformed into a neat little dining-room, a gas stove erected in any convenient recess or in the bathroom, and with paper-bag cookery, nothing more elaborate will be needed.

BEDROOM COOKERY.

For the business woman, living in one room, ordinary cooking is out of the question, yet most landladies refuse to cook for their lodgers, except at a high charge, and restaurant living is expensive. Ordinary cooking, too, means more or less heat and odours, incompatible with keeping the one room fresh and neat. In this case, too, paper-bag cookery solves the difficulty.

"WILD WEST" COOKERY.

Paper-bag cookery has been seized upon with thankfulness by a girl who went out to keep house for a brother in the "Wild West," and found the toil of cooking with rough and old-fashioned utensils beyond her capacity. So incessant were her labours, so unsatisfactory the results, that she hailed with joy and gratitude a newspaper article and some bags sent her by a compassionate relative, and now writes triumphantly that all her cookery troubles are over.

INVALID DIET.

How weary invalids get of the eternal boiled whiting and boiled chicken is well known. The poor invalid who besought his doctor's permission to have his whiting fried, and who, receiving it with the proviso it should be fried in water, burst into tears when the dish was set before him, would have been charmed with the fish cooked in a paper bag. A whiting, a chop, a fillet of chicken thus cooked are all as savoury as if fried, yet as light and digestible as when boiled.

INVALID'S CHOPS.

Trim every morsel of fat from the chop, and put it without water or seasoning into a very well greased bag. Cook it fifteen or twenty minutes according to the thickness, and serve it with any seasoning or sauce the doctor sanctions.

INVALID'S CHICKEN.

With a very sharp knife, cut neat fillets from the breast of a plump chicken; brush each fillet over with oiled butter, put into a greased bag, and cook fifteen minutes.

INVALID'S WHITING.

Choose a good-sized but not coarse whiting; have it filleted; roll up each fillet and put them into a thickly buttered bag with one tablespoonful of milk. Cook ten minutes.

INVALID'S PORRIDGE.

This may be cooked in a buttered bag alone, or cooked in a dish enveloped in a bag. Both methods are excellent. For the first, take a pint of milk and add when boiling enough rolled oats to make a batter; add salt to taste, and put into a well buttered bag and cook twenty minutes. If a dish be used, the porridge may be made thinner, and must be cooked longer, about thirty minutes. If the ordinary medium oatmeal be used, it must be soaked in cold water overnight, in a pie-dish. Next morning, add as much more water as will be needed, add a little salt. Put the dish into a greased bag and cook forty-five minutes. This porridge is not suitable for invalids, but is excellent for children.

BREAKFAST DISHES.

There are a great many breakfast dishes, besides ham and eggs which are very much nicer cooked in a paper bag.

LIVER AND BACON.

Liver and Bacon is one. Cut a calf's or sheep's liver into thin slices, flour both sides, sprinkle with salt and pepper; put into a thickly buttered bag and cook for about ten minutes. Meanwhile, have ready as many thin rashers of bacon as there are slices of liver and put them in a bag five minutes before the liver is done. Dish both together on a very hot dish and serve immediately.

BROILED KIDNEYS.

This is another very savoury breakfast dish. Foreign kidneys answer very well; skin them, cut in halves, and wrap each half in a thin rasher of fat bacon. Put them on a skewer to keep them in position, place in a buttered bag, and cook fifteen minutes.

A GERMAN BEEFSTEAK.

A German Beefsteak is very nice for a hearty breakfast eater. Mince finely half a pound of steak, removing skin, gristle, and fat; mix well with a finely minced onion, half a teaspoonful minced parsley, and pepper and salt to taste. Flatten into an oblong shape, sprinkle on each side with flour, put into a well greased bag, and cook twenty minutes. Then cut a hole in the bag, drop in an egg, and cook three minutes longer.

SAUSAGE ROLLS.

Sausage Rolls are also very good. Take four or five pork sausages, and wrap each when skinned in an oblong piece of pastry, short crust or puff pastry according to taste. Put into a well buttered bag and cook twenty minutes.

RISSOLES.

Rissoles make a nice change for breakfast, and are easily and quickly made. Roll out some light, shortcrust paste. Have ready some finely minced cooked meat, nicely seasoned, and mixed to a thick paste with gravy which has been thickened with flour. Put a little heap of this at regular intervals on half the pastry, cover with the other half and cut out each rissole with a pastry-cutter, pressing the edges well together. Put into a well greased bag, and cook twenty minutes.

BACON AND MUSHROOMS.

Bacon and Mushrooms are a favourite country dish. Half a pound of freshly gathered mushrooms should be trimmed, peeled, wiped, and put into a buttered bag with half a dozen thinly cut rashers of bacon, and a piece of butter rubbed together with a dessertspoonful of flour, a little salt and cayenne pepper. Cook thirty minutes.

SURPRISE SAUSAGES.

Half a pound of sausage-meat is rolled into the shape of an egg, and a cupful of cold mashed potato is mixed with a well beaten egg and a little salt and pepper. Cover the sausage-meat completely with the potato mixture, brush over with the beaten yolk of an egg, roll it in fine bread-crumbs, highly seasoned; put the whole into a greased "Papakuk" bag and cook fifteen minutes.

BAKED HAM.

Take a corner or gammon of bacon, or a small picnic ham; make a paste of flour and water and completely cover the ham with it, rolled out to about half an inch in thickness. Put in a greased bag and cook in a moderate oven, allowing thirty minutes to the pound. When done, paste and skin come away easily and the flavour and aroma are exquisite.

COD'S ROE.

Cod's Roe makes a nice breakfast dish. It is first boiled or steamed until thoroughly done. When quite cold, cut in thick, firm slices, brush over with oiled butter, dredge thoroughly on both sides on flour, sprinkle with salt and pepper, put into a well buttered "Papakuk" bag, and cook twelve minutes.

EGG CUTLETS.

Chop rather finely three hard-boiled eggs, add two tablespoonfuls of fine bread-crumbs, one of grated cheese and a little pepper and salt; mix well and bind with the beaten yolk of two eggs. Shape into cutlets, put into a thickly buttered "Papakuk" bag, and cook ten minutes.

EGG SAVOURY.

Chop four hard-boiled eggs, mix with two rashers of fat bacon cut in dice, pepper, salt, and a sprinkle of sweet herbs; put a slice of butter in a saucepan, add two tablespoonfuls of flour and stir together. Add slowly a gill of milk and stir till it boils. Then add the eggs and bacon and stir together till it is a thick mass. Turn out on a plate, and when cold form into balls. Put these into a thickly buttered bag and cook ten minutes.

CURRIED EGGS.

Curried Eggs are excellent, and very simply made. Hard-boiled eggs are cut in slices and put into a well greased "Papakuk" bag; a thick white sauce is made, and a dessertspoonful of curry powder is stirred in. This is added to the eggs, and the bag put into a hot oven for six minutes.

CREAMED EGGS.

Creamed Eggs are delicious. A shallow tin is well buttered, thickly sprinkled with seasoned bread-crumbs, and two or three eggs carefully broken in. Cover with more bread-crumbs, put bits of butter over the top, pour in a tablespoonful of cream, or if cream cannot be afforded, a little milk thickened with cornflour and a morsel of butter. Slide this into a well greased bag and cook twenty minutes.

Cheese savouries are particularly good, cooked paper-bag fashion. One of the most generally approved is

CHEESE STRAWS.

Mix together four ounces of butter, four ounces of self-raising flour, four ounces of grated cheese, a little cayenne, a pinch of salt, and a well-beaten egg. Roll out, cut into thin strips, and into one or two rings. Put inside a buttered bag, cook fifteen minutes, and serve with several straws inside each ring.

CHEESE FONDUE.

Well butter a dish, put into it half a pint of milk, half a cup of fine bread-crumbs, quarter of a pound of dried cheese grated, one ounce of butter, and one well beaten egg; season with salt and pepper, put into a greased bag, and cook forty-five minutes.

CHEESE PASTRY.

Cheese Pastry is a delicious morsel. Make a nice flaky paste crust, roll it out and cut into two squares. Melt three ounces of grated cheese and one ounce of butter with a teaspoonful of lemon juice. Spread this over one half of the paste, cover with the other, brush over with milk, put into a well greased bag, and cook fifteen minutes.

FRIED CHEESE.

Cut some slices of cheese, two inches long, one inch wide, and half an inch thick. Dry cheese may be used up in this way. Pour over the slices a little oiled butter, sprinkle with pepper, and leave for half an hour, turning once during that time. Make a thick batter, dip each piece in it; lay in a buttered "Papakuk" bag and cook fifteen minutes in a hot oven.

CHEESE BISCUITS.

This is a very simple but a very nice savoury. Split open several of Crawford's butter puffs, lay a slice of toasted cheese between the halves, put into a greased bag, and cook for ten minutes.

CHEESE PUFFS.

Melt one ounce of butter in a small saucepan, add a tablespoonful of water, and when it boils sift in gradually two tablespoonfuls of self-raising flour, and three of grated cheese; season to taste. Stir till the mixture leaves the saucepan, and then take off the fire. When cool, stir in a well beaten egg and set aside till quite cold. Then shape into balls, put into a buttered bag, and cook fifteen minutes in a fairly hot oven.

MACARONI AND CHEESE.

Break half a pound of macaroni into small pieces; put into a greased bag with half a cup of water, and cook for half an hour. Then put into another bag which has been thickly buttered; add four ounces of grated cheese and one ounce of butter, a little pepper and salt. Cook for ten minutes.

Many people enjoy a little stewed fruit with breakfast, and all fruits gain in flavour cooked in a "Papakuk" bag. Prunes, a recipe for which has already been given, are particularly nice cooked in this way and so are other dried fruits.

Put the fruit into a large basin, and pour boiling water over them, covering them completely. This plumps them up nicely. Cover with a plate and leave till cold. Then pour off the water, drain the fruit quite dry, and just cover with fresh, cold water. Replace the plate and leave till the morning. Then place in a large and very thoroughly greased bag, add to each pound of fruit two ounces of sugar and any flavouring preferred, a teaspoonful of lemon juice, one of sherry or of essence of vanilla or almond. Cook for forty-five minutes.

BAKED APPLES.

Baked Apples are unsurpassed cooked in a paper bag. Simply wash the apples, or pare them if preferred, put into a greased bag with a gill of water, and bake forty minutes. Add sugar to taste.

STEWED GOOSEBERRIES.

Put into a greased bag with sugar and a gill of water and cook thirty minutes. Or they may be first put into a dish and the dish enclosed in a bag. Currants and raspberries are best thus cooked. Fruit tarts and meat pies when cooked in a dish which is afterwards put into a bag, must have some holes pricked in the bag.

YORKSHIRE PUDDING.

Yorkshire Pudding for eating with meat can be cooked in a "Papakuk" bag, but must first be poured into a shallow round tin which has had a slice of roast-beef dripping or of butter melted in it. Make the pudding in the usual way; 4 to 6 ozs. of self-raising flour, a pinch of salt, two well beaten eggs, and enough milk or water mixed to make a batter about as thick as cream. Put the tin into a bag and cook twenty-five minutes.

WARMING UP "LEFTOVERS."

Paper-bag cookery is invaluable as a means of warming up cold meats. Apart from the various ways of serving up cold meat in hashes, stews, and other dishes, recipes for which have already been given, it is an excellent means of warming food which is required dished up in the same form as before.

RE-HEATING ROAST LEG OF MUTTON.

This is merely put into a well-greased "Papakuk" bag and placed in the oven to get thoroughly hot, the time depending on its weight; it will then taste exactly as if it had been freshly roasted. If part of the leg has been already consumed, cold mashed potatoes should be pressed into the space left, and shaped so that when heated and browned the leg will appear untouched.

DEVILLED MUTTON.

This is never so nice as when cooked in a "Papakuk" bag. A cold shoulder of lamb is delicious when devilled. Cut over night large gashes in the meat, and fill these gashes with dripping or butter, in which has been mixed plenty of pepper, salt, dry mustard, and a few drops of lemon juice if that flavour is liked. Leave the meat until it is nearly dinner-time, then put into a "Papakuk" bag and cook fifteen minutes.

It is the same with other joints; simply putting them into a greased bag and thoroughly heating them restores the flavour so completely that no one can tell that the meat has been previously cooked and then re-heated. This is possible only in paper-bag cookery; in ordinary cooking reheated meat is always dry and flavourless. The exact time in the oven cannot be given, as it depends on the weight; but as opening the oven door does not injure paper-bag cookery, a watch can be kept. Practice and experience are the safest guides, and the paper-bag cook will soon learn the exact time each dish requires. There will not be many failures, for a little too long will not dry up the food in the bags, and if it be underdone, it may be turned into another bag and put back into the oven. Always have the bags large enough; they may split when the food is being put in if they are a tight fit. Also, unless the bag is full large for the contents, it is somehow awkward in dishing up.

Some dexterity is required in freeing the food from the bag. If the paper is very brown, it may fall to pieces before it can be removed and bits of paper be found among the gravy. The bags should be intact and scissors used to split them open. If there is any fear of some paper remaining in the food, two hot dishes should be employed, one on which to place the bag while it is being removed, the other into which to turn the food when freed from the bag.

Many other recipes might be given, but the cook who is interested in paper-bag cookery will be able to experiment for herself in fresh directions. All the recipes in the best-known cookery-books may be worked out in paper-bag cookery, for even those which cannot be put straight into a bag without injuring their appearance—for instance, cakes of the nature of plum cake, pound cake, seed, or Madeira—can be put first into tins and then into a "Papakuk" bag with the certainty that they will gain immensely in flavour and delicacy of taste.

INDEX OF RECIPES.

Lector House believes that a society develops through a two-fold approach of continuous learning and adaptation, which is derived from the study of classic literary works spread across the historic timeline of literature records. Therefore, we aim at reviving, repairing and redeveloping all those inaccessible or damaged but historically as well as culturally important literature across subjects so that the future generations may have an opportunity to study and learn from past works to embark upon a journey of creating a better future.

This book is a result of an effort made by Lector House towards making a contribution to the preservation and repair of original ancient works which might hold historical significance to the approach of continuous learning across subjects.

HAPPY READING & LEARNING!

LECTOR HOUSE
LECTOR HOUSE LLP
E-MAIL: lectorpublishing@gmail.com